GET THEE BEHIND ME, SATAN!

A HOME-BORN BOOK OF HOME-TRUTHS.

BY

OLIVE LOGAN

(MRS. WIRT SIKES),

AUTHOR OF "CHATEAU FRISSAC," "PHOTOGRAPHS OF PARIS LIFE," "WOMEN AND THEATRES," "THE MIMIC WORLD," ETC.

NEW YORK:
ADAMS, VICTOR & CO.,
98 WILLIAM STREET.
1872.

Poole & Maclauchlan, Printers,
205–213 *East Twelfth Street*,
New York.

TO MY BEST FRIEND,
MY COMPANION AND GUIDE,
MY HUSBAND.

INTRODUCTION.

IT seems to me that there is a useful career, just at this moment, for a woman-book which shall breathe the spirit of true love, and the sweet sanctities which grow out of Christian marriage: A book which shall stand for the progressive and liberal women of our day, who love home and hate the abominable doctrines which have distracted and broken our ranks: A book which shall speak for the good and the true, and indicate the right paths of usefulness, duty, and achievement, and which shall strike home upon the loose principles that certainly are gaining ground respecting marriage and home life.

With regard to home and love—sweetness and light; our sunny parlor; our cheerful hearth; the circle of loved ones there.

With regard to progressive ideas—purity, truth, and woman's honor before everything.

With regard to all forms of error, whether merely false and feeble, or strongly gross and licentious—"Get thee behind me, Satan!"

GET THEE BEHIND ME, SATAN!

I.

DOES the poem about "The Old Oaken Bucket" strike you as sickly sentimentality?

"Utterly puerile, such a poem," I once heard a critic say; "what deeper expressions of love, what fonder outpourings of the heart could the poet have lavished on a human being, than he does on this sloppy, old, verdigrisy, dilapidated wooden pail?"

I never loved a bucket; yet I acknowledge that I am uncommonly fond of a Table.

This particular one Husband bought at second hand for five dollars—years ago, when he was a struggling young author, and was fitting up a sanctum down-town. It is a large oval table, covered with black leather—so large indeed that it was never carried in at any door, but adopts a sort of locomotion of its own and rolls in;

and it filled Husband's little sanctum so full that there was hardly room for anything else. After divers vicissitudes (there's a romantic history coeval with the ups and downs of that table, but I am not the one to tell it—no, Husband must tell you that), the old table has found its way into our dining-room, and we have eaten our meals off it ever since we bought our new house.

What I like most particularly about the table is that it is as solid as a rock. That is to say, it doesn't shake when everybody leans on it.

We have written books on it, sewed on it, ironed on it; cut patterns on it, answered letters on it, played games on it; held a fancy fair on it; married a couple in front of it. Somehow, everything that has to be done in the house gets done on that table. If any one sends us flowers, be sure they go on the table; if a new book is presented or bought, "lay it on the table." It changes its character with the hours; it is now a table of ceremony, now a dining-table, now a work-bench; the bird-cage is cleaned on the table; the porcelain tea-set is washed on the table; *boots have been blacked on the table.*

If it had been possible to take the table out walking with us, there is no question but its four legs would have had many a stretching at Central Park of a sunny afternoon. We would have it always with us if we could. It is one of our dearest friends.

And observe, that, though there are at least a dozen other tables in the house, this alone is The Table. In the front parlor is a buhl table worth as many dollars as Husband paid cents for The Table. The buhl table came from Paris, and was once in the palace of Versailles. You know how beautiful the buhl work is?—solid brass inlaid with tortoise-shell. This has four busts in brass of Marie Antoinette placed at each leg — perfect likenesses of this unhappy Queen, about as large as my hand. It is a gorgeous piece of furniture, which rivets the attention of a stranger the moment he enters the room. In the back parlor is a little gem of a table made of ebony and polished so highly you can see yourself reflected in it as you look at the delicate flowers inlaid in the top. This also came from one of the French palaces, and has thin aristocratic legs, and folding leaves that are so bewilderingly pretty that when they are up you think they look better so, and when they are down you decidedly prefer them so. Perhaps you will wonder that these beautiful articles should be in the possession of such mere democratic persons as ourselves. But you will remember that the war between France and Germany threw many choice objects in the way of cultured purchasers, and we have friends in Paris. Besides these foreign tables, there is a long list of other tables, one for every room, of course — ending with Norah's table, which Husband chopped out of the pine box in which the buhl table came across ocean, and which he nailed together so skilfully that Norah was in ecstasies over it, and when he tacked it all over with green cambric and brass-headed tacks, Norah drew in her breath and rolled up her eyes and vowed that she liked it "better than the brass Bull in the parlor!"

Husband does marvels with his tool-box, by the way. Having been reared with a pen in his fingers, he naturally finds a tool-box as fascinating as a puzzle. He goes at things with his hammer and nails on the slightest provocation, and if there is anything he can find to do with the screw-driver he is happy. He has mended the old sanctum rocking-chair so many times that it is a sight to behold. He finds a sort of comfort in having things get out of order about the house, so he can go and tinker at them.

Around The Table we gather in the evening. Husband and I, dear sisters, children, friends; puss and servants in the background; two good gas-burners over our heads; our books, our games, our needlework, our newspapers;—oh, Cosiness, thou dwellest in the Table.

Sometimes it is a round game—parcheesi, Dr. Busby, Muggins, Loto. Sometimes it is a rebus to be guessed, and all work at it. Sometimes Husband contributes an original poem, or furnishes a humorous conundrum; and frequently our Algie becomes our instructor, and tells us strange facts about fish or birds on which a learned Professor has this day lectured the boys at school. It often happens, too, that we hear him recite his lessons; and then we look at the youngster with admiring awe, as he rattles off names of rivers in China and mountains in Japan of whose existence we were profoundly ignorant.

Reader, have you a Table? No?

Then haste to get one; for, by my faith, a Table and your soul's salvation are nearer allied than you may think.

Why, reflect—putting yourself aside—upon these sweet boys and girls, now sitting around, swinging their legs and kicking sportively the legs of the Table,—which bears it meekly and does not so much as even shake in return,—how dear to them in future years may be the memory of these guileless hours passed around the Table! What a sword and shield against the hot and burning temptations of Tableless after-years!

Our boy Algie—or your boy, say—grows to manhood, launches into business—boot and shoe man makes him tempting offers—"wholesale trade, San Francisco, big thing"—he enters the wholesale trade, he goes to San Francisco, he puts to the test the bigness of the thing; it is smaller than he expected; the boy is lonely, is tempted, his beautiful face gains him wicked flatterers, his good counsellors are far away, the gilded palaces of San Francisco glitter in the eyes of nineteen, he enters "just to see;" a glass goes to his lips, he is about to take a drink, his FIRST, when suddenly the phantom of The Table rises before him, he dashes the cup to earth and flies!

Excuse me, if in my excitement over this

picture, I adopt the language of the temperance lecturer.

The truth is, Algie—typifying our boy or your boy—puts the glass down gently so as not to attract attention, whistles softly in an off-hand manner and then goes quietly out.

But he is saved, all the same; and the Table did it.

Or our girl—or yours; in a few years she will be a woman. We cannot always stay by her; she will have to meet and battle with the world as we have done. She is already greatly impressed with the idea of a larger sphere of usefulness for woman. Will it ever be her fate to fall into the hands of those emissaries of Satan who call themselves Free-lovers? Will the specious doctrine ever be poured in her young ears by oily Mephistophelian women, until, carried away by it and the passions of youth, she is on the point of falling? Why, let but her memory not die within her brain, and I will risk her, Satanesses, even in your toils! The recollection of The Table, the knowledge of the horror your doctrines inspire in the breasts of those who sat around it, will carry her pure through an ordeal even as fiery as yours.

Thus it may happen that a second-hand five-dollar table, animated by love, vivified by sympathy, humanized by daily contact, may have the power to save a living soul.

II.

AROUND our Table we strive to be all children together. *Why* is it that grown people generally consider their own physical and moral altitude so much above that of children, that when they try to unbend they do it about as gracefully as an elephant who folds his flabby legs beneath him and dumps himself down to receive his castle?

I have seen a sin-ridden man behave with such haughty contempt to a little girl—merely because she was a child—that for a moment his presumption might almost have caused you to lose sight of the palpable truth—that the little girl, being a late telegram from the kingdom of Heaven, was a thousand times more valuable than the man, a worthless express package, labelled C. O. D. for Satan.

I have seen a father come home from work,

and finding his daughter sitting in his favorite chair, cry out in a rough voice—"Here! here! get out of that! What are you doing in my chair?" As if he thought a piece of furniture so honored as to be sat on by so mighty a potentate as himself should never, even in his absence, be defiled by furnishing support to any small person.

Is not "My dear, let Papa have his chair," as easy of utterance as "Be off with you?"

What linguistic difficulties stand in the way of "Daughter, will you be good enough to bring me my slippers?" And where is the child whose eye will not brighten, whose cheeks will not flush with pleasure at the knowledge that she is her father's own little friend, "her Papa's girl?"

I once dwelt in a family where there was a Father who had six daughters. Think what a clan! But he loved them every one. Each, to him, even in earliest childhood, had a distinct character; one was classic and majestic; one, a great reader; one, thoughtful and inquiring ("wish you had a dictionary slung around your neck," said her brother Bill, "so you wouldn't be forever asking me what words mean"); a fourth was the family beauty; a fifth was musical; the sixth, the cunning little baby—born in a disastrous cholera season; therefore when she squalled the girls pronounced her "choleric."

And this father, poet, scholar, great traveller; of whom we fully believed the neighborhood stood in awe for his learning; whom the great magazines of both continents courted for their pages; was a courteous gentleman to his youngest baby.

This tells heavily, in the time to come. You may not care for this baby-critic while she is still a baby—but the day may come when she will be a baby no longer, and her opinion of you will have been formed in that very infantile period for which you had such contempt.

A child's mind is limited in its objects. It has not pored over books; it is ignorant of Latin; but it knows if a blade of grass springs up between the bricks in the yard, and can tell where the tacks are placed which hold down the carpet. A fly's eye sees a narrow territory, but it knows that territory with a minuteness that would astonish you in spite of your great goggles, many times bigger than its whole body. Thus does your child—girl or boy—see little traits in you, good and bad, which you and other grown persons overlook, being occupied with your larger fields of observation and criticism.

This home of ours is built up on love. Every room is full of it. It sings in the songs of our bird, it perfumes us through the odor of our flowers; the very cat mews it; the tea-kettle hums it; every inanimate thing cries it with a voice as ringing as an angel's trump.

At risk of seeing a smile curl the lip of yon cynic reader, I will tell you that many and many a time we gather around our old Table, set for a meal, and reach out and grasp each other's hands as we sit, in pure gush of simple affection for each other, and thankfulness to God for giving us our home. Not one cloud mars the harmony of that group. We have all known sorrow keenly; it is that, perhaps, which enables us so fully to appreciate the worth of that which we enjoy. And it is our unanimous verdict that nothing in this world, so far as we know (and our travels have been over weary miles, and in many countries), nothing can equal the satisfaction of true heart's love, and true heart's home.

Not all the romances that were ever written, not all the love-songs that were ever sung, could give the mere curious inquirer one gleam of knowledge of the perfect joy which marriage brings to the wedded couple who sit daily at our Table. Oh, the radiant beauty of that rare, rich love! How it shines and glows! How it warms every heart that comes near it, and beholds its pure, white flame! I would if I could put the love-life of these people on a pedestal, and turn upon it the blaze of a moral calcium light, that all the world might look upon it and behold its beauty, and see how its glorious effulgence flings into deepest shadow the black and iniquitous structures called Free-love, Mormonism, and the like.

This husband and this wife are true heart-twins. Their every sentiment is in common. Every desire of the one is a heart-craving to be met and humored by the other. They have scarcely need of words to communicate what they feel; to look in each other's eyes is to read the secret of each other's souls. The language they speak with their eyes is deeper, richer, stronger than any words which ever yet were framed by mortal lips.

We know that this marriage was made in heaven. Every member of our little household can see that the golden links were riveted by angels. Yet it was born of mutual sorrow. Iron is united by the fiercest flame. With torn and bleeding hearts, half their span of years gone, this man and this woman joined hands and said, "Until Death us do part."

Knowing that the sad day must come when Death *shall* part them, they hold every day that dawns upon them a blessed privilege of companionship. More precious than any molten gold is their association. Marred by no strife, dimmed by no jealousies, purer than anything else on earth is such a love as this. And they know, too, that their separation will be but for a time. What God hath joined together, He will not put asunder.

We have no gloomy beliefs, at our house. We do not think of Heaven as a dreadful, far-off abstraction, but as a cheerful and cheering reality. We believe our home-circle will be a most happy one, Up There.

Sister Rebecca has had to part with her heart-twin—Dick, her Dick, her brave, hearty, strong noble-minded Dick, stricken down by Southern fever-heats in the prime of his manhood. Dick waits for her in heaven. She knows she shall meet him. She lingers a little, by God's will, here. She speaks of him so often and in such bright and happy tones that a stranger would think he were alive, and might come in and take his seat at our Table any minute. Dick's picture, daintily framed, stands on the buffet on Rebecca's left hand; the hand of her wedding-ring, the side of her heart. "This is Dick's," she says of his belongings, as if he had them in daily use. "My pillow bears the imprint of Dick's head," she said one day as she was putting on a clean pillow-slip, "he always oiled his hair." This without any of that gaunt horror, or sentimental gloom, that most people have regarding the articles the dead have used. She patted the pillow tenderly, and looked at it with a fond smile as if she saw there the beloved face once more.

III.

I MARVEL sometimes at the presumption which made the inventors of the licentious thing fix upon the name "free love" for their abomination. It is precisely like the performance of the quack doctor who compounds some disgusting and poisonous draught and blazes it on fences and dead walls as "Elixir of Life."

The only freedom love knows is the freedom of marriage. It is common in these degenerate days to speak contemptuously of the bonds of marriage. By the way, that is a law term, is it not?—the "*bonds* of matrimony."

Rather let us have a higher-law term for this blessed thing. *The emancipation of matrimony!* That is a *truer* phrase. So much happiness, so much freedom, with so much innocence! The hearts which yesterday could not mingle without sin, to-day mingle freely and with God's blessing.

If I could fancy a "free-lover" loving with such love as that which I have just now pictured to you, I should marvel at the stupidity which would not have that love endowed with the freedom of Christian marriage. To feel that towards this man your heart yearns every hour; that towards him your whole being is drawn by strong cords which only death can break; to long to rest in his stalwart arms and pour into his ear the gush of tender, endearing epithets which wells up in your breast—and with all this to feel that the world stands between you and him and says, *This is sin!*

Is not that being in the bonds of slavery?

To repress your natural instincts; to hold back every longing; to refrain from every caress, or to stand condemned by the stern laws of a society which, after all, is based on pure morality.

To the lover with soul imbued with such love as this, Marriage comes as a blessed relief from thraldom. That which yesterday was sin, to-day is virtue! You have stood up before the world, and with your friends about you as witnesses—with sisters, brothers, father, mother, all there to smile upon your act—with the minister of God to bless it—you have promised to love and cherish each other so long as ye both shall live—and all good men and women smile upon you. Is not this freedom? In truth there is no other, for those who love.

Yes, I pity the woman who can feel satisfied to sacrifice all this. She can never know what real happiness is.

For the rest, I stand amazed at the bold assumptions of ignorance herein. They talk of love, those "free-lovers," as glibly as if they knew what love is! They have not a glimmering idea of it. The vainest young girl whose fancy is tickled with a notion that some callow youth adores her, and who knows therein as much of the true glow and glory of love as a baby staring at pictures in "Mother Goose" knows of literature or high art—this girl is yet as far advanced in the knowledge of true love as any "free-lover" who flaunts her vile creed in honest people's faces to-day.

Yes, unto me has come that knowledge which, when it comes to any soul, is seen at once to be the simple truth—that there is no *true* love which is born in a moment full-fledged. True love never did and never can exist in a union of short duration. The sentiment is the growth of years, and of long acquaintanceship.

When we were girls, each passing passion or fancy was believed to be love. *We* knew! Ah, isn't it astonishing how much we knew when we were very young? I remember quite easily the time when I should have read with Charley somebody—I forget his exact name now—such words as here are written, and laughed at them as the utterances of an old fogy.

When your day comes to be an old fogy, dear young girl, my kindest wish for you is that you may be able to lay your hand in the hand of a good man, and feel that you too have acquired this knowledge: that life is good for nothing without true love—not the wild, pestering thing which worried and tantalized your young heart years ago, but this restful, substantial, trustful love which makes you happy in the mere knowledge that *he* is with you; which makes you grateful, cheerful and at peace with all the world, day in and day out.

This married couple at our house illustrate my subject as completely as if they had been framed by my own fancy—yet, they are no more fictitious characters than you are yourself—you who sit reading this page. They have not lived a humdrum life. If you were to read their story from its beginning, you would say that no novelist ever devised a tale more thrilling, more romantic. In it is included almost every element which goes to the making of a modern novel. The scenes in which they have figured have been the most beautiful and picturesque in the world—amid the roar and rush of mighty London town; in the whirl of gay, seductive Paris; away up on the tops of snowclad Alps; among the grandeur and the glory of the Sierras; in the Rocky Mountains; in castles on the Rhine; over the fierce, arid plains of the great American desert; through the lagoons of the torrid South—where else? I might go on for pages in merely picturing the spots of earth which this man and woman have pressed with their feet, in their various roamings through their strange life-story.

After the stirring dramas of their two lives, they are now one. Look at them in their home! They are more enwrapt in each other than any Isabella and Alphonso you ever read of. No woman is so beautiful to that man as this woman—yet her first youth has gone, taking with it the rosiness and roundness of her cheek, and the crudities and inequalities of her character. To him, she is perfect—as he is to her. They read the same books, lead the same life of labor and of pleasure. Hours upon hours these people will sit conversing together, and never was there known between them one moment of *ennui*, one second when interest flagged, or when they desired other company. Other numberless hours have passed when not one syllable has been uttered; hands were busy, minds were plying on workaday affairs;

but through all, and under all, this great love lies, not like a roaring cataract, but like a broad stream on whose smooth, strong breast every earthly care is bravely and tranquilly borne. On him the woman rests; "What a brave, noble husband you have to lean on!" a friend who knew him well once wrote to her; but not less does he rest on her. I saw them last evening at twilight—none were by; their attitude was the attitude of the most romantic lovers. But, when they are in presence of other people they are as prosaic as two of the same sex. In fact, they have had five years of a strictly Platonic friendship—beginning without a thought of love, a dream of the possibility of marriage—their tenderest sentiment one of honest admiration for each other's qualities. They did not know it, but they were building their future life and love on a foundation of granite. Time rolled on, and the day came when it seemed right for them now to part. Part? It seemed so easy to do, until they tried to do it, and then they found it were easier to part the waters of ocean, and bid each half to roll its separate way. So they clasped hands and said, God has joined us together; we will obey His law.

Our dear Robert Collyer says that as God made Eve for Adam, so makes He a certain woman for every certain man; and when the pitfalls and dangers of our own wicked blindness and folly, or other people's wickedness and folly, fail to keep these people apart, then this is marriage—and nothing else is marriage, nor can it be made so.

In such a marriage as this is there any danger of pining for "free love?" When one has found a diamond, one does not wish to exchange it for a pebble, no, nor for a handful of pebbles.

IV.

HOW beautiful our Table looks to-day! Spotless napery, glittering glasses, a few appetizing niceties daintily served. In the center stands a large vase, whose broken top is deftly hidden by the sprays of some long, green plant.

"By the way, Rebecca, what is that green plant?—Oh, no, it cannot be!—*not* carrot-tops!"

"Yes," says Rebecca, pouring out the chocolate in our thin, shell-like china cups. "Mr.

Tyler, our greengrocer, was just about to cut them off and throw them under his stall; but I said, 'Never mind, Mr. Tyler, you needn't cut off those carrot-tops; I generally make bouquets of them.' He laughed at that, but you see how pretty they look. I was sorry to find Jane had broken the vase. I didn't know it before. You did, you say. It is a great drawback that Jane's daily avocations generally include the breaking of something that we would prefer to have remain whole."

Jane is our second girl. She is the finest-hued and the slowest creature, we think, that ever lived. Her complexion is as white as wax, and her hair is so light that at the temples you can scarcely tell where the skin finishes, and the hair begins. Her eyes are blue; pretty little figure; not yet eighteen. We have often tried to get at the mystery of this strangely fair complexion. Perhaps some of us muggy folks would like to have one like it. She said once that the reason of it was that she cut her feet with a stone when she was ten years old, and the blood all ran out of her body.

"But you must have some blood left," said Algie, "or you'd die."

"No, I ain't got no blood left in me body," persisted Jane; "that's the reason I'm so slow. That's the reason I break things."

Of course after this bloodless explanation we should be cold-blooded indeed if we were to think of scolding her when she breaks things. We can only wait patiently till she gets some more blood, or submit quietly, and as a matter of blood, to her daily breakages.

Jane is not very strong-minded. A mouse is a terrible animal to her. One or two large roaches nearly prostrated her with fright. Rebecca cheered her spirits, and brought her a trap.

"Now," she said, "Jane, just put that in your room, and when you hear the roaches holloa you'll know you've caught some."

"Will they holler, mum?" queries Jane, aghast at the prospect.

There is no good, sensible, housekeeping reason why we have not discharged Jane long ago. She is certainly not a prize, viewed merely as a servant. Why then *do* we keep her? In a word, because we are attached to her. We did let her go once, and she cried as if her heart would break. Then she took to making us visits occasionally, just to see how we were getting on. And one day, in a weak moment of real, kindly affection for the child (she is scarcely more), we took her back.

Yes, our love is so all-embracing that it needs must cover with its warmth every creature within our doors—say nothing of those without them.

It covers the very cat. Not because she is at all a superior character of a cat. She is, in fact, a somewhat humdrum creature, our Kittle. She has no bright ways; she is not very handsome; she has even a disreputable habit of sleeping at odd times in the coal-bin, and as a result her white coat is sometimes sadly soiled. Still we love Kittle, and it would go hard with the dog that should dare to worry her.

When she curls herself upon the rug before the grate and falls to purring contentedly, she looks so happy that we are tempted to endow her with all the feline virtues. She becomes a type of the sweet, domestic peace which is the guardian spirit of our home.

V.

So profound is my reverence for true Marriage, that my soul chafes almost unto fury at the idea of baseness in any way associated with it.

If I abhor Mrs. Freelove when she rails at marriage, I abhor Mrs. Mercenary no less when she pollutes marriage by making bargains in its holy name.

Between the woman who lives with two husbands and is married to neither, and the woman who marries the man she well knows she does not love, there is not so much choice as between a rotten apple and a sound horse-chestnut.

By all the love I bear for marriage, I protest against the pernicious errors so earnestly fostered in its name—chief among which is that error which holds a girl put into the world for the purpose of marrying a man, and for nothing else.

When you will believe, and act up to the belief, that a boy's purpose in life is that limited one, I will concede that the girl has but that one excuse for being.

But you know very well that you have ambitions for your boy. You do not teach him to consider marriage as an only end in life. To be sure, you hope he will some day marry and settle down, become a good husband and father, and an estimable citizen; but you leave all that to come about in its own good time. If this were your course with your girl, it would be better for her—and better for the boys, too.

While there is abroad in the land an army of girls, each seeking whom she may marry, your boy is in danger of being entrapped into a foolish marriage, which will make work for the divorce court later on.

Verily I say unto you—and I am no man-hater, but so far at least as one man is concerned a devoted man-lover—that men are to blame for the married flirt, for the half-starved sewing-girl, for the insolent, inefficient servant-woman. Every one of these separate branches and others like them—even that terrible one where lost souls, dragging polluted bodies, haunt the night streets, and offend the chastity of the moon which coldly shines on them—every one of these is a branch of the deadly Upas which men yearly plant, daily water, hourly tend. The root is that widespread and pernicious idea, carefully fostered by men in a thousand ways, by hints, by winks, by plain words, by actions which speak louder than words, that the business in life for women is marriage; the only girl who is successful is the girl who is engaged; the only woman whose "fortune is made" is the woman who has hooked a husband.

You, father, scanning these lines, deny perhaps that you have ever said to your daughter that her business in life is to get married. But have you ever done anything to encourage her to have any other business in life? Have you even begged her to refrain till the last moment from taking from your hearthstone the exceeding great joy which her presence brings there? Has it never happened that you have recommended this man to her consideration, and added that he was rich and looking for a wife? Have you never shut the door on that one because he hadn't a dollar? Or that one because he was not a marrying man? Have you never alluded to the expense of keeping a large family of girls? Have you never audibly wondered how Smith's ugly daughter caught rich Johnson?

Has it never struck you as amazing strange that *our* girls got no offers when *everybody else's* girls get married?

If you could place yourself in the position of a girl so situated, eating some one else's bread, wearing some one else's clothes, occupying a room in some one else's house, you would know how to feel for her. A thousand things cut her to the soul. That frown you wore at breakfast this morning—was that because young Batkins hasn't proposed yet? Perhaps you spoke of the high price of flour—nay, I do not mean that you intended anything personal by such a purely business-man remark, but it hit the tender, sensitive, self-reproaching girl at your table, who *knows* you want to marry her off.

"'It is nine dollars a barrel,' said he, at the supper-table," wrote a lovely girl to me during the war, "and I laid down the bit of bread I was eating. Another morsel would have choked me."

I have known girls whose guardians exhibited such unseemly anxiety to get them married off that every manifestation of growing admiration on the part of their gentleman friends was kept by the girls a profound secret, lest the impatient elders should rush in at the next visit, take all for granted, and ask When the wedding?

But you may say, Is it not likely that the support of these helpless girls *is* a serious burden to these parents or these guardians?

Sans doute. Nobody disputes that. Indeed, no family I know seems rich enough to bear this burden, and I know some families of tolerable wealth, too; millionaires, at least. But I would still like to find a family which is rich enough not to care whether its daughters marry, or whether they do not.

One of the richest men in New York said in my hearing once, speaking of his daughter who had passed the age at which girls generally marry, "I get *angry* at her sometimes, because she don't get a husband. She needn't bring me a poor man. I'm not going to help a poor son-in-law. No, she's a rich man's daughter, always been used to luxuries, and she must marry a rich man."

But, that is what *poor* men's daughters want to marry; and if this girl was placed exactly in the same position as a poor girl, what advantage was it to her to be the daughter of a rich man?

This same man freely gave his son one hundred thousand dollars to set him up in business in Australia; and in talking a bookful at him one day I told him that he had much better have divided that money between his children and given them equal chances for success. Fifty thousand dollars must be no small sum even in Australia where they dig gold out of the earth; and fifty thousand in New York would have enabled the girl to make the investment in a husband she desired (yes, there was the old romance—the poor lover, the rich daughter, the obdurate father, true to his rôle of stern parent) and trust to this man, her heart's choice, to get an income out of it. It seems to me, with as much money as that invested in United States bonds, a person of the poorest abilities could sit down and make a decent living out of them by cutting off the coupons.

But to return to people who really find it difficult to meet their weekly expenses, and by whom the support of an additional person is keenly felt. I say, very well; then you must take one of two positions: either say frankly that you are not able to support this girl, and take the consequence of that; or say warmly and truthfully that you are, and take the consequence of that. If the first, then help your girl lovingly and cheerfully to help herself; let her choose her career; she knows better than you do what she can do. If her talents are of no more brilliant character than will take her—as our Norah's have—into the kitchen of your next-door neighbor, place no obstacle in the way of her doing that. If they lead her to making speeches in public, blow not one breath against her for doing that.

A now-celebrated literary woman told me that her brother persistently denied her relationship with him for years, because his pride was wounded; he had not strength of mind enough to support the position concerning woman's work and wages which she boldly took in her writings. But he got bravely over it as years passed and her success grew—even to the extent of sharing her income with her in a fraternal spirit.

It is such paltry family pride as this, which does much of the mischief. There is no girl so shallow that she cannot learn to do something that would earn her bread. Nine girls out of ten *do* do, in the household where they live—for which they get no praise, no thanks, much less any pay—such work as, were it performed in any other household, would bring them bread and wages too, and both would be considered fairly earned.

I have spoken of our Rebecca—our good sister, who does us the happiness of sharing our home. She lives with us; we all live together. That is the poetic side. The practical side is that she is our housekeeper, and works hard. She is a good housekeeper, and would command her price in the market. She has never been in the market, but that is no reason why we should ignore her value. We do not. A pretty figure we should make pretending that we think so much of her, and then giving her less than persons utterly indifferent to her would give for her services! Any stranger's family who needed her services would give her board, lodging and salary. Shall we not do as much for her as a stranger's family would? We do. We give her board, lodging and salary—and love. Thus we have the advantage of the stranger's family, and not the stranger's family of us.

But if—which God forefend—our lovely home should be broken up to-morrow—its hearthstone shattered, its ashes flung to the winds—I would gladly take that dear sister by the hand and go with her from house to house of my wealthy friends, and ask them if they didn't want to engage my sister as housekeeper on a salary. No pride of mine should stand in the way of her earning an honorable livelihood. A dastardly coward I should be indeed were I, in my effort to hide my fallen fortunes, to constrain her to remain by my side lest the world should comment on her going forth to labor—the while I led her a life of torture, grudged her the bread she ate, even insulted her widowhood perhaps by urging her to marry for her bed and board! I thank my God I am no such coward.

Now and forever be accursed that pride which drives many a noble-hearted, hand-cuffed girl into an abhorred and bestial marriage! Pride of family and of purse, how I wish your father Satan would rise and claim you both for his own, and sweep you off the earth where you work such woful mischief!

VI.

HOW many or how few years ago it matters not, but it was before I had written or publicly spoken about woman's rights, or wrongs, I accompanied a beautiful girl on a strange errand. Goaded by the innuendos relating to the extraordinary fact that nobody proposed to her, while Mollie Follie had just caught a rich man —a leather-dealer in the swamp, whose sole subjects of conversation were tanning and hides —cut to the quick by references to the high price of flour, the ruinous rate of living, rent, clothing, shoe-leather, &c.—this girl found an excuse for leaving the breakfast-table, and the house.

"An early visitor, Estelle," I said to her, kissing her peachy cheek as she entered my room.

"Yes, early in one way, but sadly late in another. Please read that advertisement, cut from this morning's paper."

Wanted, a nurse-girl, to take care of three young children. One able to give some primary instruction preferred. Apply between 8 and 9 in the morning, at, etc., etc.

"What of it?" I asked.

"I am going to apply for the situation."

"You?"

A girl who lived in a brown-stone front, with —presumably—nothing to do from morning to night, apply for a nurse-girl's situation!

I say presumably, but the presumption was far from correct; the truth was that she made beds, swept floors, dusted the parlors, polished the glass and silver, and on washing and ironing days went into the kitchen and washed dishes. But all this went for nothing. If the fact was noted now and then, she was made to understand plainly that if it were not for *her* sake, they would scarcely be at the expense of living in such a house at all; if she timidly grieved that they should do this, and assured them that for her part she would be happier in a cheaper house, they made tacit answer that such houses were the best places in which to catch rich husbands; that really skilful girls did catch such husbands with such houses; that Mollie Follie had just done so. She (Estelle) had been taken to Saratoga, Newport, Long Branch (the very last places to catch a husband!); she had passed a winter in a gay city hotel; and finally she was in this house. How much longer were they to wait for the returns of this heavy investment?

If you ask me if thus much was said by Estelle's aunt and uncle, in so many words, I answer—Probably not. But, it was there; that was the atmosphere she breathed. The air had been especially charged with the offensive gas that morning.

"What can I do for you, dear?" I asked, laying down my pen.

"Come with me, please. I confess I feel somewhat timid. But I will go—whether you come or not."

A long ride in a stage, and a long walk westward across the avenues, brought us to the advertised house. It was not such a fine one as that in which Estelle lived. I confess my heart beat a little faster as we mounted the steps; as for Estelle, her lips were livid, but they were tightly set.

We asked to see "the lady," and were ushered into the parlor. Why not? We visited in better houses than this.

The lady soon appeared, smiling and extending her hands, mistaking us for friends as she advanced from the sombre depths of the back parlor. As she drew near she saw her mistake, and, seating herself, gave a polite glance of awaiting our pleasure to tell her the object of our call.

At this moment my eye rested on Estelle, and though many and many a time I had admired her from the depths of my heart, and thought her the loveliest girl I ever saw, yet never in my life had I seen her looking at once so beautiful and so elegant as now. No detail of her appearance escaped me; and at this moment, though years of sorrow and suffering have elapsed, chasing away many beautiful visions of the past, I can yet see her peach-like face set in the frame of a soft gray velvet bonnet, a delicate moss-rose lying on the parting of her luxuriant hair, her long eyelashes shading her downcast eyes. She was dressed from head to foot in soft gray poplin, with perfectly fitting gloves of the same shade; the gold band bracelets she always wore clasped her wrists; and her muff and fur collar had been recently bought for seventy-five dollars.

I might give you an idea of how this toilet was got together without great expense. Such a girl is generally a mistress of expedients. The effect of Estelle's costume was that of great expensiveness. But the dress was an old one of her aunt's made over; the furs were a long-promised present from a distant rich relation; the bonnet was her own handiwork, thrown together out of a handful of discarded materials; the gloves were new. Her aunt had bought them with a groan and thrust them upon the unwilling recipient a few days before. It was not her dress, however, but her attitude, which was so striking; as she sat there in all her glorious beauty, utterly reposeful, utterly determined, almost sanctified in her stillness and her resolve.

"I have come to apply for the place of nurse-girl," she said sweetly, lifting her pure eyes steadily to the lady's face.

Please imagine the expression of this latter! If a bombshell had burst in her parlor she could not have been, apparently, more astonished. She looked at me, she looked at Estelle, she looked at herself. By all odds, Estelle was not only the handsomest and the youngest, but also the wealthiest looking person of the trio. The lady was rather untidy in a dressing-gown and slippers; I was in my working dress—a substantial English linsey, suited to the labor which deals with ink-bottles and dusty libraries.

There is no use giving the conversation in detail. The coolest person present was Estelle. The lady could only reply in broken snatches of sentences.

"But the wages, such a trifle!—seven dollars a month."

"They include board and lodging. I will take them if you are satisfied with me," said Estelle.

"But have you ever taken care of young children?—washed them, dressed them, walked them out in the street? One of my children is a baby and must be carried, or pushed in a perambulator."

"I could soon learn how to do these things," said Estelle, with exceeding sweetness and modesty. "And I like children."

Here I put in a word about her great amiability, her gentleness, her refinement; but all this was written on her face. The lady hesitated. It was evident she feared there was some deep mystery here; some plot, some plan, some Wilkie Collins imbroglio of which she was to be the victim. That so simple a thing could be, as that the girl had sought the situation to do honest work and get an honest livelihood in return for it, apparently did not strike her as probable. Yet her womanly heart was touched. She was strongly tempted to say yes.

At that moment the front door opened with a latch-key, and an instant after, a man's form stood on the threshold of this parlor. It was easy to see he was this lady's son. He was fashionably attired, and had an all-night air which spoke of champagne suppers and other dissipations.

At first the lady smiled on seeing him; then she looked at Estelle, and then her brow clouded.

The young man after glancing admiringly at Estelle (who would not have done so?) turned and went up stairs.

As for Estelle she had not heard his step, and had not lifted her eyes.

The lady spoke up sharply. Her whole manner had changed.

"Well I'm sorry, but it is impossible for me to take you. You are too young. You will not suit."

Nothing remained but for us to take our leaves. We took them.

If that lady should read this book she will not learn from it who Estelle was, but it may surprise her to learn the name of the person who went to her house with a friend to help beg a nurse-girl's situation.

I have formed many theories about her sudden change of manner. The wildest, and therefore the one which lingers longest in my memory, is that she connected—in some way known best to herself—the beautiful applicant for the nurse-girl's position with her dissipated son, and resolved at once that she would have no wool pulled over *her* eyes!

I never broached this suspicion to Estelle; it would have caused her unnecessary pain.

When we had turned the corner, and were out of possible view of the lady or her son, we stopped, and took our bearings. Then I observed that Estelle's lip was quivering.

"Is it not dreadful that I cannot get a place even as child's nurse! Oh, what an unlucky girl I am! What was I born for? Nobody cares for me—nobody wants me!"

Spite of her efforts, some hot tears fell. I

think several of the passers-by saw them. But, dear me! a wretched, broken-spirited girl is no novelty in the streets of New York.

"Being amateurs in this business," I said, "I am inclined to think we made one mistake. You are too well-dressed—you look too much like a lady. One would think that ought to be a recommendation to a mother who has little girls growing up; but it is marvellous how people's minds run in the old ruts. She wants an Irish or German nurse-girl of the orthodox pattern; and when she has got her, she will pass half her time in abusing her, and the other half in wondering whether the nurse isn't abusing the children. But, no matter. Rome wasn't built in a day. We live and learn. Let us now go where a lady-like appearance and good clothing are a recommendation—to the retail stores."

With an interval of but ten minutes to eat a sandwich in a baker's shop we passed the whole of that day in unsuccessful efforts to get a place in a "store." Everything was full. It was dusk when we stopped, almost completely baffled; and we were as tired as hounds after the chase.

"There is only one thing more," I said; "I have a friend who has an influential position in

Nip and Tuck's Sewing-Machine Establishment. She may be able to do something for you."

We were not far from the place, and found them just bustling about before closing for the night. A few words from me made my friend understand my errand.

Well, she said, they were full now (the old story); but a vacancy might presently occur; in fact they *might* make one. She would speak to Mr. Tuck, the junior partner.

He came. He was favorably impressed. He said they always wanted their young ladies to be nice-looking ("Did he presume to mean a compliment?" said Estelle, afterwards); but, one thing every new-comer must understand, and that was:—that she had got to recognize, that she had got to *believe* that theirs was the finest machine in the market. She had *got* to believe that; otherwise she could not impress customers with that belief. It *was* the best machine, he declared stoutly; no machine that ever was put together could do the work or stand the wear that their machine could, and as for the stitch, it was by all odds the finest stitch ever seen. Any girl who came there with a prejudice in favor of any other machine was not wanted. He might as well say that first as last.

Estelle had always used that which is the best known of the machines, and to which Nip and Tuck's little affair compares as a tea-kettle to a locomotive.

"For the first month," continued Mr. Tuck, "we give no wages. Our young ladies are learning to operate" (meantime an inducement to customers was, that *they* could learn to operate *in an hour!*); "and when they know how to operate we give wages according to the ability of the operator."

"How much do you give to a good operator?" I asked.

"Well, we give some of our young ladies seven dollars a week."

"Seven dollars!"

"Yes, but those are our best-dressed young ladies. We expect those young ladies to dress very well. And then we seat them by the windows. We should be glad to have this young lady sit there."

The shop was on a corner, and was one sheet of plate glass, so to speak, from floor to ceiling, on both streets. Everything and everybody inside was as plainly visible to the outside throng of Broadway as if the machines and the girls were out on the sidewalk.

Estelle shuddered, as she glanced at the huge show window where she should be expected to sit on exhibition; but, without referring to that, she said, in her candid way,

"But this stitch ravels the whole length if you pull the thread; how do you explain that to customers?"

Mr. Tuck seemed to get greatly excited whenever the stitch the machine made was in question. He grew quite red in the face, and said loudly:

"It's an advantage! Tell 'em it's an advantage. Who wants a machine where you have to cut every stitch in ripping? Besides, it only ravels one way. You can't ravel it the other."

He pulled on one end of a couple of bits of cloth which were stitched together; this resisted, and he looked triumphant; but as he finished his experiment, a loop at the other end caught on his watch-chain, and ripped the seam the whole length before you could have said Jack Robinson.

Estelle drew me aside. "It would be utterly

false on my part to say I believed that stitch superior to that made by the machine we use at home. It is only good for millinery work, or for light fabrics which are not to be washed. How can I tell a falsehood?"

Will you think me a wicked counsellor? My feet were sore from standing and walking in my hitherto fruitless efforts to aid this girl to escape from the degrading position she occupied at home; I was hungry, I was tired, and I knew that her sufferings and discomforts were greater than mine. I begged her to be diplomatic; to try to manage matters so that she need injure neither her conscience nor her interest, and take the place.

After stipulating that she might sit with her back to the window, and that she was to receive seven dollars a week after four weeks' apprenticeship, Estelle concluded to come. She had resolved in her heart that if the hour came when she must tell a falsehood, she would resign her place; meantime, it had not come, and it might not; and she was making a beginning in self-support.

I left Estelle listening to some final remarks from Mr. Tuck, and sauntered slowly to the door talking to the lady through whose kind interest this arrangement had been made.

In another instant Estelle brushed past with her face aflame. She grasped my hand.

"Come, please," said she, "I shall not take this situation—cannot—must not."

Before I knew it the glass doors were closed behind us. My last glance through them revealed to my eyes in the dusk, which the busy lamp-lighter was fast dispelling, Mr. Tuck shrugging his shoulders, half angrily, half contemptuously.

Of course, I thought that he had insulted her.

But I did the worthy Mr. Tuck great injustice in thinking so. In declining the place, Estelle had no doubt greatly insulted him.

She did not wait for me to ask her what had happened. She spoke:

"Where in the world do you suppose he wanted to send me to-morrow—with a machine?"

"Not to some den of iniquity?"

"To Mrs. Wickersham's."

"Who is she?"

"Don't you know Mrs. Wickersham? One of the richest ladies who visits at our house—Aunt Sophia's most stylish friend. She would die of anger and shame if she were to find out that I had gone to Mrs. Wickersham's."

"Did you not contemplate these probabilities when you resolved to cut loose the bonds which chafe you so?"

"I did not contemplate the probability of my going as a machine girl with another machine girl to Mrs. Wickersham's house, where I have been a guest."

"And will you please tell me," said I, almost out of patience, "whether Mrs. Wickersham, a heartless, soulless woman, ignorant and narrow-minded, given over to dress and show, who pretends to admire you—I remember her now—more than any girl she ever knew, and yet who wouldn't give you a dollar to buy your dinner to-night—"

"I don't believe she's got a dollar to give," said Estelle interrupting, and thereby breaking the smooth flow of my torrent of indignation.

The vision of this wretched Mrs. Wickersham, without a dollar to call her own; the poor, weak appendage to a rich man, who hung a pair of three-thousand-dollar diamond ear-rings in her ears, not out of compliment to her ears (which received few enough compliments from him, according to her own story), but as an advertisement of the enviable condition of his whiskey-filled pocket-book, fairly sickened me with sorrow and disgust. And yet, if Estelle could have made such a marriage as this Mrs. Wickersham had made, her Aunt and Uncle would have thought she had attained the grandest glory this mundane sphere has to offer woman, and would have rejoiced thereat exceedingly.

Estelle returned to her old life. Worn out, tired, discouraged by her long day's unsuccessful tramp, she felt the noble resolves of the morning fade away in the darkness of the falling night.

You say this was a very weak girl. I say she was stronger than the average, or she never would have made even this spasmodic effort to free herself from a position which she loathed. It required no small amount of courage to go to a strange house and ask for a nurse-girl's place. It was trying beyond words to tramp for a whole day from store to store, and shop to shop, and meet rebuffs at all.

It seems strange, but I believe it to be strictly true, that the persons who had in their hands the direction of the life-journey of this immortal soul, truly loved her. Nay, I *know* this to be true; yet I concede that they come under the head of those people who love, yet have "a mighty queer way of showing it." Their efforts to get her married were unselfish. All they wanted was her good, they said. They had no object but to have her make a marriage worthy her; but their idea of worthiness in a man related principally to the state of his pocket. But if she had married a millionaire they would not have expected nor touched a dollar of his income—thus far, they were noble. Meantime neither the millionaire, nor the semi-millionaire, nor the demi-semi-millionaire, nor even the non-millionaire turned up; they found the supporting of her weary work and let her see it; but when she suggested doing something for her support —oh no, their pride forbade that! So the deadlock continued. She returned to the glorious career of waiting to be married.

"And I don't see why she shouldn't get married off-hand, if she was so beautiful, amiable, and estimable as you represent her."

Thus I fancy some easy-going, good-natured masculine reader saying.

—Well, that is precisely what her Uncle and Aunt used to say.

VII.

A MOST joyous period to a girl is when she says good-by to the trammels of girlhood, and "enters life" as a woman; when she first wakes to full consciousness of her beauty; when she begins to realize the power of that beauty over the opposite sex; when she sees clearly that beauty is a crown and sceptre to its possessor, and makes her, while it lasts, a queen.

I say "while it lasts;" but this consideration rarely presents itself to a girl's mind. She hears sermons preached about the fleeting character of beauty, but she does not apply them to herself. She goes home from church, looks in the glass, sees that her cheek is as round and her eye as bright as they were six months ago, and she thinks this prognostication does not apply to *her*. It is, perhaps, true in a general way, but she is going to be an exception.

You tell her that homely Mrs. Smith yonder was once as pretty as herself. She shrugs her shoulders. You think so if you say so, but you are mistaken. You have old-fogy ideas on the subject. You are arguing from the ten-or-twenty-years-ago point of view, when lots of frumpy, horrid things were in fashion. And Mrs. Smith's beauty must have been of a piece with coal-scuttle bonnets and waists up under the arm-pits.

There appeared on the book-stalls a few years ago a little volume called "The Autobiography of a Beauty." The story in its pages was scarcely more than a catalogue of the number of men whose brain had been turned or whose hearts taken captive by the loveliness of the face and form of the autobiographer. Duels had been fought, "knock-downs" come to pass in hotel corridors and other public places, between men maddened with the beauty of that face, and fighting for its smiles.

And that the reader might have some idea of what this face was, a fine steel engraving of it was placed opposite the title-page.

Oh, how entrancingly beautiful was that face! It was the style of beauty which we used to see in the old English volumes called "keepsakes," which, full of engravings of beautiful women, were laid on drawing-room tables in place of the photograph albums which we now find there.

But this face was so *very* lovely! You scarcely wondered it had driven men mad. Soft, loosely-twisted brown curls fell gracefully on each oval cheek; the fine brow shaded with the rippling locks which strayed carelessly across it; the nose a perfect aquiline; mouth a rosebud's self; chin small, round, firm; neck like a swan's; shoulders sloping away gradually into the perfectly moulded arms; waist tapering in beautiful symmetry with the rest of this fairy-like vision.

I should not have been so minute in this description of this picture if I had not something further to tell. The original was well known in New York and Boston society. Yes, the autobiographer, the Beauty, walked among us, a thing of life. And when her book appeared with that title, and that picture in it, such a shout of derision went up among the belles of the period as is seldom heard from lips usually well guarded against all vulgar, unrestrained expressions of emotion.

For the lady as we knew her was enormously

stout, her enormously large waist wider than her enormously wide shoulders; her face red, mottled, blotchy; her hair dragged off her exposed forehead in that most trying of all fashions, *à la Chinoise;* her throat large, full, short; her chin, a double one; her walk, a duck's waddle. And yet—will you believe me?—to the eye which *looked*, the original of the picture was plainly to be seen in the present face.

Every one knows that no complexion is so easily reddened and blotched as the most delicate and fair one; no hair breaks and tangles so easily as that which is soft and silky. The eyes were the same, the nose was the same—it was the Beauty—with her beauty gone.

There was nothing humorous to me in the sight of this woman, formerly so lovely. She was a living Sermon, more prophetic than minister ever preached. To look at the picture and then at her, was like looking at one you love lying in the coffin. To this complexion you must come at last.

There is a ghastly picture in the Wiertz Gallery, at Brussels, which I sometimes wish—in my indignation at the frivolity of those girls who absolutely worship their own beauty, ay, bow down and worship it, offer up incense to it, make a very god of it—I sometimes wish, I say, that I had power to invoke this picture to appear before me when I listed, that I might hold it up to the view of these girls and strike terror to their hearts with it. It is the picture of a beautiful girl in the high bloom of health, her cheeks glowing, her eyes sparkling, her ruddy lips parted, coming across in a museum the skeleton of a girl labelled "*The Beautiful Louise!*" She stops before it, and is contemplating it with deep and solemn thought. Perhaps it is a girl she knew; one of her schoolmates, it may be; her sister, even. Look how the hollow sockets return her gaze! See the grin on those bony jaws, in ghastly mockery of her look of sad interest! They are both of a height, these two; the breast bones of the skeleton indicate the same form of bust as that which is so admired in the living girl; every bone, every joint, every articulation is there—Oh, they are sisters, if only in the sense that we are all members of one family! The resemblance between the two is perfect. One is a living skeleton, prettily clothed in flesh; the other is a dead one, with its clothing gone.

And this was the beautiful Louise! Where is her beauty now?

I yield to no one in my admiration of beauty, but I place it in the right scale—far below mind, not to be mentioned beside heart attributes, soul qualities.

One of the most striking characters in Dickens is Mr. Carker, the man who has beautiful teeth. Now we all know that beautiful teeth are much to be admired for their mere beauty's sake; many an otherwise handsome face has been spoiled by blackened, decayed and offensive teeth; many a homely face with a large square mouth has been redeemed from positive ugliness by a splendid set of really handsome teeth. And handsome teeth have a worth beyond beauty; unlike the fairness of one's cheek, or the shade of one's hair, sound and handsome teeth are necessary to health.

Mr. Carker has so exaggerated in his own mind the beauty of white teeth, has fixed so entirely erroneous a value on the beauty of good teeth, that he goes through the world in which he moves with the idea ever present in his mind to show you his teeth, his beautiful teeth, his very-superior-to-yours teeth, his worth-more-than-anything-in-the-world teeth. It is a curious comment on the value of his possession that he proves to have nothing but teeth; his heart and character are worthless.

Girls, you who read this page, drink deep these truisms: that Beauty is but skin deep; that handsome is that handsome does.

These inelegant phrases strike you as forcibly as nursery rhymes would, perhaps; yet like many of the latter they have the kernels of sound philosophy beneath their grotesque husks.

Greenough the sculptor told me that his services were once engaged to make the bust of an American girl. He had not seen her before she came to him for sittings; but her mother said to him, "You'll find my daughter is a very pretty girl, Mr. Greenough, except that she has a *bad skin.*" The artist naturally thought that the young girl's skin was disfigured; pitted, perhaps, or blemished with some eruption. He was surprised to find that her skin was as smooth and as soft as velvet, but that it was yellowish in tinge.

And remember, Miss Strawberry Cream, that you cannot long keep that youthful glow; the apple blossoms are more delicate and fresher than your cheek, yet they change into round, ruddy apples—not half so charming in a mere æsthetic sense as the blossoms were, but more appreciable in solid value.

A bit of undigested food ; late hours ; I know not what triviality, may any day turn that fresh rose in your cheek into a faded one. This is making no allowance for serious illness, which is liable to attack you as well as the next girl, and may come any minute and change your whole appearance. Happy indeed are you if, when a malignant fever strikes you, it robs you only of your fine complexion, leaving your hearing and your eyesight as perfect as before.

So much for the beauty which is skin deep.

Has it never happened to you to have acquaintance with a person whose physical beauty was undoubted, yet who gradually developed qualities which aroused your disdain and disgust to that degree that you shuddered at the sight of that person, and loathed their very beauty?

For a magnificent exposition of the growth of this feeling, read "Romola," by that gifted woman "George Eliot." See how the noble-minded girl Romola is fascinated by the gorgeous beauty of the youth Tito; observe how she invests him with all the lovely attributes of mind and heart which *should* go hand in hand with such a winning face; follow her closely as she discovers that not one of these attributes is in reality there; that he is vain, selfish in the most supreme degree, heartless, fickle, faithless, lying, hypocritical, and a traitor; till at length her heart closes against this one who formerly lived there, enthroned a king with a crown of her own conjuring, not with one he really possessed; and she shuts him out forever. His very beauty had grown into ugliness for her.

Thoreau rendered "Handsome is that handsome does" poetically; he said,

"We are all sculptors and painters, and our material is our own flesh and blood and bones. Any nobleness begins at once to refine a man's features, and meanness or sensuality to imbrute them."

VIII.

CLARA VERE DE VERE goes to a ball to-night. Her toilet is lovely; delicate violet and white, just the faint tinge of mourning which Clara has put on for that uncle of hers in California who died three months ago and left her money. Clara is one of the few very rich girls of America; with large estates and revenues all in her own right, left her by different members of the rich old Jersey family to which she belongs. Perhaps you think there is no disadvantage in being a rich girl. Clara could tell you her troubles! One of the chief among them is that she never knows whether people really like her, or whether they pay court to her on account of her money. Another is that if she wears an elegant dress and the diamonds which are heirlooms in the family, she hears comments about her always wanting to outshine other girls "because she's got money." If she wears a simple dress, folks say she's mean.

"Did you ever!—a white tarletan! such a rich girl! Oh, they say she's awfully stingy; I pity the man that gets her!"

Every artist she meets expects her to buy his pictures or statues forthwith, because she has money. If she doesn't, again she is dubbed "mean." That she may not want them, is nothing to the point; she might give them to some of her friends. Tickets for concerts, church fairs, lectures, piano-forte recitals pour in by the score for her purchasing. If in any case she declines, the fact is noised about from one aristocratic house to another. Her defenders say she's eccentric; her defamers that she's stingy. People lean forward to see what she puts in the contribution-box; tradesmen double their prices when she sets out to buy of them.

Fashion gossipers report her in print as engaged to this man or that. There is no privacy for her anywhere. She goes to a watering-place, and every eye is on her. People of questionable standing follow her as she walks, and stop when she stops, to give lookers-on the impression that they belong to her party. Other people make her trumpery presents, expecting something gorgeous in return; and if she does not send it, they set to work to defame her again.

Clara is a coquette. How she is to discover whether a man truly loves her or not, she says she does not know. Meantime, she amuses herself with that most dangerous of all diversions, flirting. Look at her at the piano, surrounded by admirers! see how she asks—with winning smile—this young officer to turn over the leaves of her music-book for her; and as soon as the leaf is turned, casts her eyes towards another gentleman and sings, gazing at him pointedly (or so it seems to him), "*toi que j'aime!*" Ah, Clara, Clara Vere de Vere, better let the foolish yeoman go! You're spoiled, incurably; you are that most terrible thing, a rich coquette!

But, coquetry thrives in every circle of young people, and in every condition of purse. I have seen negresses out in the fields planting cotton, arrayed in pannier overskirts and jockey hat and feather, tossing their heads coquettishly as some dusky admirer neared the fence.

Here is our little friend Susie—a dreadfully coquettish girl of sixteen. She goes to school, daintily clad, tripping along on tiny boots which she declares don't hurt her—and I suppose she knows. She has a small regiment of admirers. "My paper collars," she calls them. They are the boys of the neighborhood and range in their ages from fifteen to twenty.

"They always go and do something when they are twenty," says Susie; "generally marry."

We ask her how she likes that.

"Oh, I don't care; there are always new comers to fill up the gaps."

Pretty precocious, eh? Yes, she is a girl of the period. She'll get no better till she gets worse—that worse being the final coquetry which leads to a foolish marriage.

Susie's principal field of battle is the sidewalk. She asks permission demurely as a kitten of her mother to walk up and down the sidewalk at dusk with a girl-friend. She receives it, and they start off so innocently—oh, cat's whiskers and cream, butter wouldn't melt in their mouths! All at once they are joined, first by this boy, then by that, and the first the astonished mother knows, looking out of the parlor window, is that the two girls are the extreme centre of an advancing wing of a solid masculine army which stretches from curb to area gate.

It is difficult to put a stop to an amusement, a diversion, an intercourse which seems so harmless as this; yet such pranks are dangerous.

Why, can you believe that our Algie—not yet fifteen—has got a lot of notes from a girl of his own age or near about, tied up with blue ribbon, and put away carefully in his trunk tray? I disapprove of this, but what can you say when he invites you to read them, and you find they are composed of such harmless nothings as:

DEAR A.

I got ten for writing to-day; did you have your grammar lesson? Yours truly,

LULA.

Or this:

Miss Lula Lawson's comps. to Mr. Algernon, and requests the pleasure of his company at a party on her steps this evening.

N. B. You are requested to bring something.

P. S. Mottoes—or anything nice—would be acceptable.

"This is a jolly country for an unmarried man to live in," said to me not long ago a young Englishman who had been in America some months, "because the girls are so jolly fond of flirting."

"Do you find them any more so than English girls?" said I, prepared to wave an imaginary stars-and-stripes over his head, and dare him to the fray.

"Oh yes, you know; positively—you mustn't feel annoyed—young ladies most delightful young ladies—not the slightest harm meant, you know; quite as irreproachable as our English girls, but they do things, you know, that would ruin the character of any young girl in England."

"As what, for instance?"

"Why, meet a fellow."

"What do you mean by 'meet a fellow?' You surely do not mean that you are acquainted with young girls in this city, or this country, who claim to be reputable, and yet deliberately meet young men!"

"Yes, I do. They don't mean any harm, and there is no harm done. If they weren't reputable—I assure you I've too much regard for my own repute to go and meet *them*."

"If such conduct on the part of any girl were known, it would call forth the severest comment, I am sure," I said, tartly.

"If it were known positively that she had come to meet me—or rather that I had come to meet her—it would not be thought right, of course. But I meet her accidentally, so far as any one knows; and your American custom permits girls to walk the streets alone; nor does it find any impropriety in a gentleman's walking home with her; or in their even taking a few turns up and down Broadway, or on the Avenue."

But, from such small tricks as these grow the very worst social sins which curse our large cities. From these grow the vain, foolish, useless wives who crowd these cities; grow many of the miserable tragedies which spring from such folly and uselessness.

"If our girls were reared on the French plan," said a lady to me the other day, "these things would not happen. In Paris, a girl dare not go walking in the streets without a proper *chaperon*. You know that, I presume?"

"Yes—by personal experience."

"Indeed!"

But I cannot agree that the way to remedy this evil is to restrict the liberty of the girl in a matter so inherently innocent as walking in the streets. I will go to a great length in the matter of personal liberty. What men may innocently do, women should be equally innocent in doing.

The cure for coquetry is not in any Rareyan system of tying up the feet. If you cannot approach the heart of any American girl that lives through sincere and kindly appeal to her sense of honor, your experience is sadly different from mine.

I would gladly welcome the day when communion of the *soul* and *mind* were as free between men and women as it is now between men alone, or women alone. Indeed, such communion is necessary, to pave the way to a truly happy marriage. A courtship of five years where the parties have never seen each other, except at church, or surrounded by the prim gentilities of the girl's mother's drawing-room, is less likely to make each acquainted with the true character of the other, than seeing him or her subjected to a month's attrition out in the busy world, and bearing with or chafing under its trying ordeals.

There is a class of large-minded, well-educated unmarried women of a certain age, whose years and whose talents should protect them from any such injurious and insulting comment as "Guess she's pulling her cap for him!" when they see fit to hold converse—brief or lengthy—with kindred minds of the opposite sex. But, taking into consideration what a large amount of human nature there is in very young men and very young women—how greatly human nature predominates over science, metaphysics, or philosophical deductions !—I think it safer for young girls to err on the side of old-fashioned maidenly reserve. Therefore I hold it best that even an accidental meeting between a young man and a young woman shall result in no long walks, no perambulating of Broadway or the Avenue. Steer straight for home, girls, or say "*Bon jour!*" with a curtsey to your cavalier, and continue your shopping expedition alone.

As for the Parisian plan which decrees that an unmarried girl, or even a young married woman, shall not so much as run across the street without being accompanied by an elderly relation, or a male or female servant tagging behind her, I look on it as a sort of petty tyranny.

When I first went to Paris I was a girl of eighteen, but I was perfectly self-reliant, and, knowing enough French to make myself understood, and above all to thoroughly understand what was said to me, it never entered my head that I needed any escort. In such broad, light, airy and well-guarded streets as those of beautiful Paris, what need had any man or woman of an escort in the daytime?

My first day out ended in an adventure. I had walked far, and stood long, looking in at the shops with all their tempting displays. Glancing at my watch, I found it was late. I started for home.

When I reached the Boulevards, a large body of soldiers was passing. I stood and looked at them for some time, as company after company filed by. As troops, they were gorgeous; but dinner was a more attractive prospect at that moment. I was tired and hungry. I wished they would pass, and let me cross the street; the number seemed indefinite; and on and on they came. I was growing desperate. "The first break there is, I will run across," I said to myself.

Presently there came a break, and I ran across. The whole column burst into laughter. One man caught me by my shawl (they were walking fatigue-gait, and so not keeping step) and cried out "Hahahaha! When a delicious-little-very-superior angel like this runs in front of the military, they kiss her! Oh, but certainly! Else what good to be returned from the Crimea, with medals and glory? Hahahaha! commencing by the officers, all the military, they kiss her. *Allons!* Let us commence! One, two—"

Before he could say "three," I had pulled my shawl from his grasp, and fled like the wind in the direction of my lodgings. My blood was boiling! I gasped forth the story of my indignity when I got home. Old Madame B. was there.

"But the harm is with you," said she. "*Mon Dieu!*" and her shoulders went up to her ears, "Is it sufficiently incomprehensible how these foreigners act? My child, what thou dost in thy savage New York I know not, but here, let me tell thee, it is not *convenable* for a little one of thy age, eighteen years—Mon Dieu, nothing but eighteen years!—to be walking the streets of Paris alone! The military naturally supposed thee a child of the people, a grisette, some little Nothing-at-all! What will you have! All alone—in the streets of Paris—and not the least suspicion more aged than eighteen years!"

Spite of this harangue, I could not make up my mind to sit sucking my thumbs in a dark apartment on glorious sunny days in beautiful Paris. I had nothing to do, and an escort was not to be had, for men are busy as elsewhere in

Paris with pleasure or profit; and go out I would. I was always plainly and modestly dressed, and walked along with the timid, reserved air that is natural to eighteen—or ought to be.

I was strolling along the Rue de la Paix one day when a price-card on a necklace in a shop caught my eye. One hundred and fifty thousand francs! "Thirty thousand dollars," I said to myself. I was always amusing myself in changing imaginary francs into air-drawn dollars, and the reverse. "Now, who in the world," thought I, "can afford to pay thirty thousand dollars for a necklace?"

I leaned close to the window-pane, and riveted my eyes on the dancing beams of the great white diamonds. They were superb. But even at that age I was too practical to feel any desire to possess so costly a treasure; and I remember thinking—and thinking a smile with the thought—that if I had thirty thousand dollars, or twice that, no part of it should go to purchasing so useless a bauble.

My reveries were interrupted by a voice—a voice in which there was a certain quaver which tells but one story—age.

"Wouldst thou like to have those fine things there?"

I turned and saw a wizen-faced old man. He was scrupulously dressed in the highest fashion; elegantly gloved; perfectly booted—evidently a Frenchman of the best class of society. But he looked like a wrinkled dwarf out of a fairy tale, to me; and his question chimed with my fancy.

I looked at him without speaking. No one else was by. When I had surveyed him from his face to his feet with amazement, and then returned from his feet to his face and stared at it with more amazement, he spoke again.

"Because if thou wouldst desire to find a well-beloved dear-friend—oh, but he would spoil thee, go! Some fine dresses, a cashmere—is it handsome, a cashmere?—also to the jeweler's one would hasten. Ah, when a little *girlette*—under twenty I am sure—has a sweet face, the eyes of an angel, hair all gilded, it is very annoying to be clad in an ugly robe quite past the mode."

It was my best dress, if you please, he was alluding to in these complimentary terms.

Still I said nothing. And perhaps this may

astonish you. But you must remember that I was as nearly "thunderstruck" as people generally are, when they say they are. I don't exactly know what it is to be thunderstruck. Where I came from the lightning strikes, and the thunder applauds. Else whence those "thunders of applause" we hear about?

Bear in mind, too, that I was not fluent in the language. In fact, I was so astonished that I couldn't think of the first (or last) French word. What I *felt* like saying was this: "Oh, you red-faced, old, white-headed scamp! you ugly, frightful, French, frog-eating dandy! ain't you ashamed of yourself, trying to make a fool of me, you absurd old Mephistophelean Faust, you!"

Those being my sentiments, I naturally found some difficulty in expressing them.

Will you believe that this old pest—a Decorated of the Legion of Honor, he told me, proudly pointing to the ribbon in his buttonhole—who made remarks on my best gown—actually cost me two francs?

Yes, I had to take a cab to get rid of him. He walked after me. Oh, I was savage! When he found I'd beckoned to a cab, with true French politeness he sprang and opened the door. I shut it after me with a bang, and leaning out I cried, half choked with angry tears,

"Oh, you nasty old thing!"

Perhaps thinking I was bestowing some parting words of politeness upon him, he waved his hat above his head with a graceful swing; and the last I heard he was calling on the Virgin to protect me, and reminding me that fine clothes were handsomer than old ones, and that he himself was none other than Monsieur le Baron de Croquemitaine, ancient Officer, Decorated of the Legion of Honor.

If I did not speak of this episode at home, it was because I believed that both of these adventures were purely accidental, and that they were no index of what must inevitably happen to a young woman walking the streets of Paris alone.

Shortly after this I was walking with my guardian. At the Church of the Madeleine he prepared to leave me; he was going to his club, I to visit the family of the excellent Monsieur Vattemare. Oh, that lovely French home! Oh, the superb old man Vattemare, enthusiastic in his efforts to establish—that which he did establish—an International Book Exchange with America, thus filling Boston public libraries with priceless volumes! Oh, the dear old mother! fat and happy, working worsted on canvas, as it seemed, forever. Oh, the curious *Abbé* son, and the loving, amiable daughters, my companions! Were Parisian sins and follies fifty times more prominent and ghastly than they are, the recollection to me of that one peaceful, calm, happy home were enough to nullify with its virtue and goodness all their evil.

My guardian had no more than taken a step or two away from me when behold the same wizen-faced old man who had so excited my indignation in the Rue de la Paix.

"Ah ha! Once again the good Virgin throws us together, Sainted Marie be praised!"

That was enough. I turned and ran as fast as my feet would carry me, and caught up with my guardian, who had turned a corner.

Of course he was furious; and after that insisted that I should have a man-servant.

The duty of this personage, who was easily found, at a high salary, was to walk behind me; and when he did so no one ever spoke to me, or treated me otherwise than with the highest deference. That cockade and those white gloves; that black suit and that fine straight figure, were very effective upon observers; but they bored me terribly sometimes.

In the first place, as I was a foreigner, Pierre seemed to feel it necessary to point out for my observation and admiration buildings with which I was entirely familiar. Walking along about two yards in front of him, I would hear a voice crying "Madame! Madame!"

"What is it?" I would say turning quickly, expecting something important had occurred.

"Madame will be pleased to observe that this is the magnificent church of the Madeleine. It takes eight men with outspread arms to compass one of those pillars. It is modelled after a Grecian temple. Inside—"

"Thank you, Pierre. I am perfectly acquainted with the church of the Madeleine."

Sometimes I would look behind me, and find that he was missing. On such occasions I would stand still, looking about me anxiously, wondering if the earth had opened and swallowed him, when presently he would come rushing out of a wine-shop near by, his cockaded hat a little set on one side, and his irreproachable white gloves slightly soiled at the finger-tips.

"Mon Dieu!" he would cry, with the most innocent expression of face, "why, where could Madame have escaped herself?"

I could hear him tell other servants whom he met, and with whom he exchanged a word, that I was "Madame la Marquise;" sometimes my rank would take a leap, and I would be "Madame la Duchesse;" and once, when I had an expensive new outfit, it was "Madame la Princesse" whom he had the honor to serve.

IX.

SPEAKING of expensive outfits, have you ever visited Long Branch, and seen the over-dressed little girls whom injudicious mothers thrust into the parlors in the evening at that vulgar place? Is it not a painful sight?

One summer there was one child whom I observed particularly. She was an exceedingly plump girl of about twelve or thirteen, and her bedizenings were worthy of a duchess. Her hose were silk, her boots were of delicate satin or gilded leather, her dress was of rose or blue taffetas covered with Valenciennes lace; her jewels were coral or turquoise; her flowing hair was artificially crimped; her full bosom and plump arms were bare; her lower limbs were exposed like a ballet-dancer's. Every evening her truly idiotic mother saw this infant sailing through delirious waltzes in the arms of an extremely tall officer of at least twenty-five, and instead of trembling at the sight, smiled complacently at the proud knowledge that, so far as dress was concerned, her daughter quite literally outstripped the other children present.

And it is easy to observe that these noble feelings already have large place in the little girl's throbbing bosom. Her eyes—ringed around with black streaks of dissipation—flash with delight as she observes the undoubted superiority of her toilet.

Her manners are offensively presuming. In a quadrille for which grown people are taking their places, she spies a position which suits her fancy, and rushing up to it edges those who occupy it away.

She poisons the whole atmosphere of girldom. All the other children must have silk hose and gilded boots; if they haven't they envy the wearer, and imitate her ways as nearly as possible. She coquets with the tall officer whose sword-belt is higher than her head; she giggles behind her fan; gives a boy of fifteen a rose out of her bosom; and, over there in a corner, a grown man is showing her tiny glove (which she has given him) to some ladies who laugh.

She is the subject of conversation between a couple behind me. They are French, and speak in that language.

"*Elle sera séduite!*" says the man.

"Undoubtedly," answers the woman.

What a comment on the harmless pranks of a girl of thirteen! I turn and look at the speakers. They are a distinguished and elegant couple. They are judging her coolly, calmly—but from the French stand-point, I am convinced, and so I take the liberty to turn and tell them.

"Our American manners are quite different from the European."

"That is evident!" says the lady pointedly.

"This young girl, I trust, will grow to womanhood, judge for herself the qualities of the men she meets, choose a husband, marry and live a virtuous wife."

"Have we the honor to speak to a friend of her family?"

"No. I do not know who her family is, not even their name."

"She is a daughter of the celebrated gambler X.," says the man, twirling his moustache. "One is not a saint. One has lost many little hundreds at his faro."

A gambler's daughter! In the olden time to be the daughter of a gambler would have ben considered a position of moral and social death. But it seems we have changed all that. She is the head of this circle of children, the queen of the set, and is followed by the children of people bearing honorable names. The modest and pretty daughter of the President of the United States is standing there in the group with her. Her gambler lineage seems to be no great drawback.

In dress as in most other things the extremes are not admirable. While gamblers' wives and daughters (though by no means these alone among our women) occupy the one extreme, they are quite as near my idea of the desirable in dress as are those self-styled reformers who would sacrifice all the graces of attire on the altar of their ism—even as the free-lovers would sacrifice the graces of home on the altar of *their* ism; the difference being strongly against these latter, of course, who are shamelessly wicked, as well as æsthetically unlovely.

If I pity the little girl who has a rash and foolish mother who permits her to be dressed as the gambler's child was dressed, I also pity the little girl who has a too timid and rigid-minded mother by whom all elegance in dress is tabooed.

With all our love for the little ones, we think too little of their small world and its ways. Your world of trials, troubles, anxieties, jealousies, fears, hopes, and joys has its little counterpart in the child-world in which your daughter lives. If you think she is a creature without emotion you are much mistaken. She lives, she breathes, she feels, she likes, she dislikes; be satisfied if you can keep her back for a few years from those masterful passions, loving and hating. Let her dress be neat and clean, and to some extent at least, near the prevailing fashion. These things lie deep in many a child's soul. Ridicule in the mouths of children is to other children so bitter, so unsparing!

I remember when I was a girl, and going to school, that the cape of my new sun-bonnet by a mistake was made too long, and my mother tore off a few inches of it, and then sat down to hem it up again for me. But before she "stuck the first stitch" she was called away. For three days there was confusion in the house; sickness, departures, arrivals; the hemming of my sun-bonnet was quite a long job; no sewing-machines in those days; and for three days I wore that unhemmed sun-bonnet to school. It seemed to me I never was "mad" and "didn't speak" so frequently in my whole school life as during those three days; and the hole in my armor being the lack of hem to my sun-bonnet, the girls speedily found it out, and thrust their daggers in it.

"Ahh! What a sun-bonnet! Why don't somebody hem your sun-bonnet? Eh? 'Father sick, sister gone away, and mother hasn't got time!' Then why don't you wear your flat? 'Haven't got a flat!' Say, girls! She hasn't got any flat!"

Chorus of voices, and fingers outnumbering those of the witches in Macbeth pointed towards me in derision.

"Ehh! No flat! Why what do you wear on Sundays? Why don't your mother buy you a flat? I guess it's because she's too poor—ehh!"

With that the sun-bonnet was snatched off my head, and flung from girl to girl with laughter and contempt.

My darling mother never knew what I endured through that sun-bonnet. She will learn the story of it for the first time from these pages. She hemmed it calmly when she got time, and I am thankful—for it is strange how well I recollect every detail of this trifling circumstance—that I forbore to tell her all I suffered.

This lesson is clear: never force your child to wear a garment which she has reason to believe will bring her into ridicule with the little world by which she is surrounded. If you will not buy nor make her something similar to what other little girls are wearing, she must needs wear the obnoxious clothing, for she cannot go naked. She is in your hands; you are her mistress; she your slave; but she will chafe under your proprietorship as all bondmen do, and will count the hours till the time when she shall be a free agent.

This brings me to a subject on which I have already spoken and written quite freely, but about which there is always a word to say. I mean the question, What shall a woman wear?

The women who as many as twenty-five years ago set on foot the movement which claimed suffrage as a woman's right, made, it has always seemed to me, a vital mistake when they associated that movement with eccentric notions of dress. Grant, for argument's sake, that the dress they desired to introduce to supersede the one which for centuries had been in vogue among women, was beautiful, useful, economical, healthful, and appropriate; argument aside and truth to the front, it was only a few of these things. It was called, you remember, the Bloomer costume. The excellent Mrs. Bloomer, with whom I have the pleasure of being acquainted, denies with some warmth having been its originator. She says other persons devised it and wore it, long before she ever thought of it; but believing it to be a wise reform she advocated it in the columns of a newspaper she was then publishing, and by this means her name got tacked to it.

It is an undoubted fact that many women spend much more time and money on their clothing than they can afford. It cannot be denied that many fashions, pretty enough in themselves, have been exaggerated by women of poor judgment, fond of *outré* styles, until they have become offensive to the eye of taste. But even at their worst the dresses now worn are less ungainly, less unsightly, more poetic, more modest even, than the stiff, hard-lined, cast-iron Bloomer costume. Scarcely a day passes that we do not hear or read some denunciation of woman's dress, its absurdity, its extravagance both to eye and pocket; but the truth is there never was a period when so many sensible ideas were carried out in the clothing of women as at present.

I trust that it is something more than a fleeting fashion which decrees, as it does at the present writing, that tight-lacing is old style, *passe de mode*, not to be thought of by a woman who pretends to fashion; that women's boots shall have thick soles, and a heel which lifts them out of the mud or snow.

Not many years ago nobody but grandmother wore a dress the waist of which closed and opened in front; then every woman in the house—except Gran'ma—from the girl five years old to the mother of the same, with daughters of all ages intervening, had to be "hooked up." And what a process it was! I have hooked the dresses of my elder sisters and those of my girl friends when my fingers have ached for an hour after. As for the victim, she was as red as a lobster while the process was under way. "Hold your breath!" was the common injunction from the hooker to the hooked. Without bated breath there was no such thing as dragging together these monstrous instruments of torture. Very frequently hooks and eyes burst off during the strain, and then a slovenly sight often met the gaze. Underwear—sometimes not too clean, for women had not the facility for making these garments then as now—was to be seen gaping through the crevices between the hooks. No woman could dress without aid; sometimes the men folks of the family had to be called in. Their strength generally succeeded in this pleasing work when every woman in the house—servants included, often called away from the wash-tub to hook up madam and enable her to show herself—had tried and failed. "I've got weak wrists; my fingers aren't strong;" these were the excuses heard.

Contrast this with the easy-fitting waist-body of to-day, buttoned up the front in two minutes by the fingers of the wearer. Shall this improvement go unnoticed?

And the shoes worn by women in that period —you remember them, I suppose? Paper-soled gaiters, laced at the sides, the uppers made of some rotten stuff—prunella, was it not called?—leather was seldom or never used for women's shoes. Heelless, the woman's foot sprawled ungracefully as she set it to earth, and a week or two's wear burst the eyelet-holes of the boots, and the untidy view from the exploded hooks in the dress-body was repeated on the inside of each foot.

And who can compute the number of early deaths which have been caused by these two follies! Many a woman has dropped dead from tight-lacing; and many and many another has dragged on a miserable existence for a few years to die of consumption at last, from only one drenching received when she was wearing these paper-soled shoes.

I have seen women come home after being caught in a rainstorm so wet you could wring them; their dresses dabbled a half a yard high, and flapping about their heels; their shoes so saturated that water exuded from them at every step. If the water-proofing process was known then it was not applied to women's cloaks. To carry an umbrella was considered an unheard-of clumsiness by dainty belles in the good old days, when, according to some authorities, "women used to dress sensibly." In this summer of 1872 not a fashionable woman walks the streets whose parasol is not equal to affording her shelter in case of a rainstorm. Of course, also, it is a far better protection on hot days than the trumpery "sunshade," about as large as a dinner-plate, which used to be in vogue.

Away back further than the days I speak of,—before America was settled by civilization's women, in Elizabeth's reign, and before that, too,—if you examine the costumes of fashionable women you will find nothing so practical, so comfortable, so commonsensical, as the dress worn by such women to-day.

The pannier and the chignon have been carried to excess; but a draped overskirt is a feature in Greek statuary and Roman painting. Next to her elocution, Rachel, the tragedienne, gave her most studious attention to the fall of her drapery. And the heads of women are tidier far to-day than when—like that of Rogue Riderhood's daughter—their loosely twisted back hair was forever tumbling down.

"The waterfall and the hoop-skirt are to a certain degree unshakable successes;" said a merchant to me recently; "and it is so because their utility is undoubted. With the first, a lady's hair is dressed in five minutes and stays so all day; putting her bonnet on and off does not disarrange her hair. This you see is a great point. And the hoop-skirt does away with the number of starched muslin skirts which must otherwise be worn to give a graceful contour to the dress. Of course, such skirts are both heavy and expensive, and therefore undesirable."

As I don't wear a waterfall myself, I can

champion the thing without being suspected of selfish motives. I grant some waterfalls be hideous—but there are some women who have a talent for making anything hideous; and therefore that is no argument against a good thing.

Were I a luxury-lapped lady, with nothing better to do than to keep myself sweetly beautiful—to trim my eyebrows, and bathe my lips in lavender water, and play the rôle of a mermaid

> "With a comb and a glass in her hand, in her hand,"

I should like very much to sit combing my "long hair" by the hour, of lazy afternoons. But as I am a woman with something to do, and for at least half the year am rushing about the country, getting up at unearthly hours in the morning, bowling over hundreds of miles of railway every day, and all the time under vigilant observation by those critics of literary women who are on the look-out for signs of untidiness — I sometimes grow weary of my back-hair and sigh for a chignon. In wild moments I dream of cutting off my hair *à la* Never-mind-who, and joining the noble army of the short-haired. But the chignon dwells most in my mind.

Here comes Rebecca. Let us see in what way reform could go to work at her costume. She is dressed in the freshest of half-mourning suits; the underskirt just clears the ground all around and is quite plain; the overskirt is gracefully raised on the sides, and the folds thus made are fixed in place with dainty rosettes of the same material; the waist is fastened with buttons up the front, and is so loose that as she heaves a deep, life-giving breath Rebecca declares that it "don't touch her anywhere." A dainty frill or ruff of snowy tarletan encircles her throat. Her dark hair, with just a few threads of gray in it, is rolled over two hair-pads which make a fine back-head, as the artists call it. Across her brow a coronet braid is laid, and is vastly becoming. This false hair is one of the things you rail against; but dear Rebecca is one of the staid-est and soberest of women, and she approves of these harmless little adjuncts. We mention Bloomer costume to her; she raises her eyes in horror. "That," she says, "would really be the absurdity—the vagary—not what we wear at present."

Do you urge that this costume of Rebecca's may be pretty, but it is expensive? It is a common black and white calico. There is no cheaper wear for women. It was made by a dressmaker with no reputation for style who lives in the Sixth Avenue, and is cheap. The neck-ruff was made by Rebecca herself in ten minutes time. For fifty cents she bought enough tarletan to carpet our back yard. She will make ruffs for herself and for all of us—she will draw out ruffs no more countable than the eggs from a conjurer's hat. She will wear that calico dress this summer without washing—next summer with frequent washings—and the next summer—well, it will not be wasted, be sure of that. She will use it herself in the early morning when she is dusting the knick-nacks in the parlor, or perhaps she will give it away, nicely mended, perfectly wearable, to some poor woman or girl. And remember, that during this summer at least, and if it doesn't get too much faded the next also, she will put on that dress and with a neat black bonnet and a pair of black gloves and her black parasol she will "walk dat Broadway down" without the least compunction; proving once more and in spite of all cavil that this is the age of true freedom in dress, when Rebecca's black calico may pass muster perfectly well on the gayest street in the world, and excite not the least sneer or other comment though it jostle silks and grenadines innumerable on the way.

There may be persons who say that the Bloomer costume was invented—not in these days when women's dress is more sensible than formerly—but in those very other days of which I have been speaking when women laced their lives away, and for the sake of small feet wore death-dealing, paper-soled gaiters.

But the railing against dress still goes on; it is a never-ceasing source of complaint. I cannot believe the objections raised then were any stronger than they are now.

"Now just see how lovely Lucretia Mott dresses!" said a dress-reform woman of past fifty to a peaches-and-creamy girl of eighteen in my presence. "She dresses sensible. Why don't you dress like her?"

The idea of the mob-cap and poke-bonnet of Lucretia Mott—a semi-angelic Quakeress of

seventy years of age—on the head of this rosy springy, merry, light-hearted girl of eighteen who didn't hesitate to sleep in the martyrdom of curl-papers for the sake of having ringlets the next day, and who spent a great deal of her loose change in buying black velvet ribbons to tie about her throat to set off the whiteness thereof—was so ludicrous that both the girl and I laughed.

"Oh, all the world knows how frivolous you be in regard to dress, Olive Logan," said the elder lady, tartly.

My frivolity in regard to dress may be plainly stated as a settled belief, that so long as Youth is beautiful, joyous, undimmed by care—and pray God that youth may be always thus, for manhood and womanhood cannot be !—so long as the savage woman gazes admiringly at herself and twists bright beads in her locks and watches the charming reflection of herself in the brook ; so long as civilization's girls have advanced no further from the condition of the savage woman than to look upon a mirror as an essential part of the furniture of their rooms (black Sarah Hoggins required a looking-glass in the kitchen as well as her bedroom) ; so long as Blondina knows that blue becomes her, and Brunetta prefers a delicate yellow—so long will Bloomer costume reforms, and Quaker bonnet reforms, fall on arid soil where fruit cannot and will not spring up.

The Friends know this well enough, and to their sorrow. It is not the pure and beautiful religious doctrine inculcated by these really good and lovely people which drives away hundreds of their youth every year. It is the austerity of their laws concerning that which touches the æsthetic faculties of every human heart. It is the lack of music, of sweet pictures, graceful statuary, harmless humorous books and conversation; and it is also the rigorous decree which forbids the wearing of raiment tinged with the hues which God painted on the rose and dyed deep in the violet eyes of the daisy.

Yes, the woman-suffrage women made a *vital* mistake in joining on to a movement which related specially to the social and intellectual status of woman a side issue—more prominent because more tangible, more immediately to be put in practice, than suffrage—which related to such a comparatively trivial matter as the cut of her clothing. Fancy a political party of men which should urge as a prominent plank in its platform the abolition of stove-pipe hats and the substitution therefor of good sensible sun-bonnets! This is an idea I have frequently made use of in speaking to audiences on this subject, and it never fails to excite laughter and applause, called forth I suppose by the ludicrousness of the simile. Yet I put it on record here as the first and perhaps best parallel which comes to my mind for the efforts of reformers who want to link "dress reform" and the ballot for woman. This in spite of the fact that I personally was never fond of dress, and am growing less and less so every day. Yet I know well enough how to enter into the feelings of a girl of sixteen; and if I can succeed in putting into the mind and heart of that girl noble ideas of woman's duty in life, higher aims than gossip and ball-going, an earnest appreciation of her worth as a soulful heir to immortality, queen of the household on earth, a power in church and state, I may well afford to leave her her pink muslin dress and her Roman scarf. I shall do violence to her instincts, if so please you, in nothing; and I challenge you to try your plan with a dozen girls while I try mine with another dozen, and if yours haven't all run away I warrant me they'll be as fine a party of female Uriah Heeps as were ever turned out to disgust a practical, frank world with their hypocritical "so umbles!" so little fond of dress, so unselfish, so self-abnegating, so far removed from any of the wicked pleasures of this sinful world, so unlike in fact what youth, beauty, health and high spirits should be—and what, thank Heaven they are! spite of Bloomerites and other unlovely angularities.

X.

I SOMETIMES hear women in small towns and villages and in the country say—"John and I were in New York last spring and stopped at the Greatenormous Hotel. How delightful it is there! How I wish it were my lot to live from year to year in such a hotel—as women do there; with nothing to do from morning till night but dress themselves and look nice."

Oh, miserable plaint, born of tyrant pots and kettles, how sad a lot it would be for the utterer, could her prayer be answered!

Let us spend the day with one of these women, as her friends and acquaintances often do. Arriving soon after her late breakfast we shall probably find her small room looking very attractive. It is well furnished; true, its proportions are contracted. It is up many stairs, but there is generally an elevator in which to mount. There are no books here, of course; there is no room for them anywhere—not in the chamber itself, nor possibly in the heads of its occupants. The bed is trimly made, but passing near it you observe that its odor is not freshly sweet; clean linen is not lavishly bestowed on permanent boarders, and to have this room—her only one for sleeping and reception purposes—made tidy at an early hour, the bed must be made before the vapors of last night's occupancy can escape.

You wonder where this woman with her many elaborate changes of dress can bestow all her belongings. There are trunks about, to be sure, but it seems inconceivable that any permanent person should submit to that wretched fate of travellers, "living in trunks;" should daily perform those most irksome jobs, packing and unpacking. But you see that her trunks are full to the brim, and to show you some new finery she will go down on her knees and unpack and repack a chest as big as a boarding-house refrigerator. She has a wardrobe too, and by that I mean the article of furniture so called. See, the door swings open; how crammed it is with hats, caps, coats, skirts, boots, shoes, slippers and dirty linen! What a nightmare such a place must be! Of course it is impossible to keep it in order. It is the catchall for everything. The room is so very small; and at any sacrifice it must be kept ostensibly in order.

Now glance at the lady occupant of this room. Her toilet is elaborate. Her husband has been gone to business these two hours. She did not breakfast with him. She never could have got herself up in proper style for the breakfast-table soon enough for him. So, long after he has gone, she has stuck her last hairpin, given her nose its last dab of powder, thrown one of those detestable suggestions of concealed untidiness, a "breakfast shawl," over her shoulders, and lounged in to a late breakfast.

A number of unappetizing and unhealthful little dishes are placed before her, and she takes a forkful out of one, a spoonful out of another, munches a pickle, holding it between her fingers, disposes of a plateful of hot, heavy cakes running over with cloying "syrup," drinks two cups of strong tea or coffee during the meal, and a large glassful of icy cold water after it, and then strolls with a pace like a snail out of the dining-room. She may have the "Morning Trough" in her hands, and glances idly at its closely printed columns; but she is really interested in nothing on earth except clothes, so the paper—superficial and vulgar as it is—has little attraction for her.

She is charmed to find you in her room; of all her pleasures, one of the most delightful is "talking." But this word has a limited meaning with her; it signifies chattering scandal, or discussing the exact width of a flounce, or the shade of an opera-singer's last new toilet. It means pulling down the reputation of her dearest friend, or carping about her husband's faults, or regretting that she hasn't money enough to buy more clothes, or glorifying the appearance of some gambler or quack doctor who is stopping in the house.

You try to bring up some better topic of conversation: you speak of the last new book, the last new picture, a bright, strong, helpful sermon you have recently heard, now to be bought in printed form; but she knows nothing of these things, and you see plainly that she does not want to know.

Finding her at the end of her resources, you leave her. Absolute waif on the ocean of life, useless chip floating hither and yon, what would it matter to the world at large if this minute she should sink out of sight to rise no more? Her husband would miss her, you say; we shall come to that presently.

As it is she finds the hour high noon; the reproachful sun once more at his zenith, showing her a morning absolutely wasted. But that is nothing new to her. It is the story of every day. And, what is worse, the afternoon is to be more profitless, if possible, than the morning. Another hour before the looking-glass sees her ready for the promenade. Now it is lunch-time; but she has no appetite. She has just breakfasted. She saunters out. Her gait is slow; she stops every ten steps to gaze into some shop window and long for its contents. By and by she reaches a New York museum, and here she may enter free of charge.

A museum of statuary, painting, historical relics? Oh, no. One of those large dry-goods stores which have no parallel in the world; and which tell a truthful story to the thinking mind —a bitter story of the Nothing to Do but look after Something to Wear of American women. Even London—"not a city, but a nation"—shows no such Dress Palaces. And Paris "magasins" are but small in comparison.

With a tide of other women she sweeps in through the plate-glass doors, and becomes the Torture you have read about, who bids tired clerks drag down and open to her view hundreds of yards of silk, dozens of shawls, scores of boxes of hosiery, piles upon piles of underclothing; and leaves this counter to fly to another, only to quit them all by and by and repeat the performance at another shop, coming away from all without having purchased anything anywhere.

And her reason for not purchasing is a pretty good one. She has no money. Open her pocket-book, and ten to one, you'll find barely a 'bus fare in it. She has never known what it was to make or to own one single dollar. Every penny she has had in all the years of her life has been given her as you would give a penny to a child. Her husband pays her board—or runs in debt for it; he feeds and lodges her—and when she wants a new dress she goes against her listless nature so far perhaps as to sit on his knee and twine her fingers in his hair, and kiss him, and tell him of some lovely goods they have at Stewart's. If this is ineffectual, she tries crying and whining, pouting and sulking, and one or the other of these plans generally carries the day. In this noble manner she obtains her clothing; and when she has obtained it let her not fail to give thanks and praise, as if it were an act of the grandest generosity on the part of her "lord and master"—fitting title to express the position of such a husband as this.

And when she has got her dress and put it on, who is to admire it? Not her husband, for he is away all day, and generally goes out in the evenings to play billiards, or see his business acquaintances in the rotundo of the hotel. She airs it before the women, and perhaps carries off some petty triumph there; but this does not entirely satisfy her, and she looks about for other admirers. She need not look in vain. All men are not busy; that is, during her waking hours.

Considering that he is a gambler (but that is not considered, for it is not known), and is up all night, Captain Frothingale looks remarkably well during the hours he paces Broadway, and stares at pretty women by the score. How does it happen that this married woman is so intimate with this dubious-looking man? She does not bow to him when her husband is with her. Perhaps to avoid answering this very question: How did she make his acquaintance? Who knows? I confess I don't—I can only make a guess in the matter. Perhaps by her answering "just for fun" his matrimonial advertisement, also inserted "for fun" in a newspaper; perhaps by his treading on her toes in a 'bus or street car.

"Treading on her toes!" That is a funny way to scrape up an acquaintance!

Granted. But it was the way a man employed with sister Rebecca when she lived in Brooklyn. That was before we kept house, but all boarded around wretchedly separate. By some strange coincidence, sister Rebecca would very often find herself next to this man in the Fulton Ferry and Fifth Avenue stage downward bound; let her sit where she might, before the journey was ended he would contrive such changes as brought him next her. Then he would tread on her toes. Well, put this down as possibly an accident. On the ferry-boat, there he was. She hurried to an obscure corner; he followed her and trod on her toes. In the Brooklyn cars he was there, and his accomplished purpose was to tread on her toes.

Now, Rebecca is not a silly, coquettish girl; she is a noble woman, dressed in widow's garb, modest and uncityfied. But, really, when a man keeps up a two weeks' course of toe-treading the most unsuspicious woman will begin to notice it. She might indeed say, Well, in the 'bus it was an accident; on the boat it was a curious coincidence; but the car turns the scale, and proves to her that it was an intentional plan—he meant to tread on those toes, and he intended her to notice it. Even if for one or two or three times she remained in doubt, a daily toe-treading will obtrude itself on the most prosaic imagination. And how did Rebecca put a stop to this underhand means of expressing admiration, this underfoot method of saying "I wish to know you,' this toe-pressure, which was an insult, an indignity? By remonstrance?—by appeal?—by virtuous outburst of indignant womanly language? Not at all. By merely paying him off in his own coin. By simply returning toe for toe. An eye for an eye, a tooth for a tooth, and a toe for a toe. The first time he came near her after her resolution was taken, she gathered up all the strength in her body, and concentrating it in one foot she trod on *his* toes till he howled. It was an unsuspected advantage that he had corns. He never toed again.

I think it was the wisest thing she could have done to express her contempt and disapprobation. It not only rebuked him, but it was so grotesque a revenge that it completely destroyed the puerile effort at sentiment he was making. And to think of prim, shy Rebecca doing it! Verily a good woman is equal to any emergency—even the unexpected one of having to toe the mark in this manner.

By some such means has the acquaintance between Captain Frothingale and the married woman I was speaking of been made; or they may have been introduced by some irresponsible person.

I do not exaggerate when I say that a full half of the women who are lodged in harem-like hotels, with nothing to do from day to day, week to week, month to month, but dress and look pretty, are carrying on a more or less guilty flirtation with some such person as Captain Frothingale.

It is not in France alone that married women have lovers! The acquaintanceship may end with nothing more harmful (though this is bad enough) than a few love-notes and some lavish gifts of flowers; or it may terminate in blood and disgrace, or a bullet in the seducer's brain, a lasting stigma on the woman's fame, a trial for murder, and a verdict of justifiable homicide for the husband.

But has this woman no children, you ask—no baby to occupy her time and attention?

Baby! Great Heavens, you silly creature, what are you talking about? What does *she* want with a baby? What will she do with it?—how support it? It is as much as they can do to meet their expenses now. Her husband's weekly earnings (their only income, for the wife earns nothing) are barely sufficient to pay their weekly board, lodging and laundry bills. Every dress, every hat, every pair of boots or shoes, is an emergency to be met by desperate effort, as emergencies are. How can they contemplate the expense of a nurse and baby? Oh, no, it is not to be thougnt of!

Besides she don't care for babies—in fact, hates children. A baby would spoil her figure first, and make her look motherly afterwards. So the ungodly slaughter of an innocent takes place. Hush—sh! These are bold words—bad words! Are they as bold and bad as the deed?

And, observe, the harm these women do—not by this one act, but by the general tenor of their lives—is not to themselves alone, but to the sex. Men see these women—they are prominently in the eye of men—they live in the panorama of the streets much more conspicuously than the few women whom business occupation calls there—and men form from them their estimate of womankind in general. Doing this, it is easy to imagine how low that estimate is.

XI.

ONE of my favorite illustrations of the Bœotian stupidity of some women—but this requires facial illustration to make it entirely successful—is an observation of the lives of certain wives of New York Legislators at Albany.

Every year the experience repeats itself. Those legislators' wives (each with a big cluster diamond ring on her forefinger) dress themselves in the morning in vulgar, rattling silks and point-lace collars, and after each meal they go and sit in the parlor of the Rataplan House. Whether they have been guilty of that unpardonable vulgarity, getting up from the table with their mouths full, or whether they have cribbed a few rasins or figs or apples is to me unknown, but certain it is that they are always chewing. And as they sit at the windows with dull, expressionless eyes, motionless figures and lips that for hours never open (for they never speak, even to each other), the resemblance to a cow chewing its cud becomes so strong that an active, energetic woman feels like rushing up and shaking them, just to see if they will moo.

Or a mixed Tennyson flies to her brain, and she longs to scream out:

> Legislator's wife, who are *not* Vere de Vere,
> If Time be heavy on your hands,
> Are there no beggars at your gate,
> Nor any poor about your lands?
> Go, teach the orphan boy to read,
> Go teach the orphan girl to sew,
> Pray Heaven for a human heart, and

don't sit there any longer gazing into that apothecary's shop opposite, when you have already counted a hundred times over every bottle of Derry Pavis's Hair Killer, and Humbug's Fluid Extract of Blue Jew.

The arrival of the legislating husbands creates a diversion. It has been said that you may legislate till the cows come home. These have legislated till they came home to the cows.

It is such women as these who point the moral and adorn the tale of those talkers and writers who inveigh against the helplessness of wives, the mill-stone-around-the-neck character of women in general. Yet the very men who make these observations would be the first to frown down any efforts at self-support in their own sisters or mothers; even in the women they really purpose marrying.

One of the best-hearted men I know has for his excellent wife a lady who was before her marriage a saleswoman in a store. Now you cannot think how it annoys that otherwise sensible man to have his wife refer to that period of her life; he begs her in semi-humorous, semi-pathetic tones to "Sink the shop;" but she will not. She says the shop kept her from sinking once; it may be her life-preserver again, and that of her children.

Nor does her husband see the least connection between her shop-life and her wife-life. Yet there is one; yes, and a close one. The very qualities which made her a desirable saleswoman, and which she developed by years of trade-life, are now brought in play in her husband's home, and conduce to his comfort. It is the punctuality which was imperative at the store, which makes her husband's breakfast daily ready at the minute; it is the acquired habit of standing long on the feet (sometimes carried to a cruel and unnecessary extent in stores) that enables her to keep about when other women would be on their backs. It may be in part a natural gift (but if so it has been improved by her necessary computations at the store) which enables her to add figures with surprising rapidity and exactness, and thus save many a penny from cheating or mistaken hucksters in the market-place. Her trained memory, too, makes her her husband's date-book. "Nellie, when did such and such a thing happen?" And so exact and reliable is she that if she forgets once, he, who forgets always, is disappointed and astonished.

In painful contrast to the idle women who sit chewing their cuds in Albany, or gallivanting in Broadway, or living in the Harem hotels in New York, are the thousands of poverty-stricken women who are stitching their lives away in making clothing at health-ruining prices for merchants who sell them to the first-mentioned class at purse-ruining prices. The sorrows of these girls, the swindles put upon them, the death in life they endure, have been so terrible, so palpable, so sinful that something like an organized and systematic effort has been made to protect them from the devouring wolves who employ them.

And yet, at what cross-purposes do we not work? If you ask me What is one of the most difficult things to do I know, I will truthfully answer, To obtain the services of a sewing-girl in New York city. I stand ready at the present moment to pay a neat and dexterous sempstress two dollars and a half a day and provide her board also, to make up my summer clothing; and for the life of me I cannot find her. I am obliged to wait for a girl who is engaged three deep.

I confess there is something here I cannot understand.

(Yes sir—I have read your explanation; your extremely logical, very reasonable, altogether heartless explanation—and I don't understand it any better than I did before, thank you!)

This is in spite of the fact that sewing is the favorite trade for women, the one in which more girls are employed than any other known: it would be difficult to say why, except that it is a career for women approved by men—perhaps because, being so laborious, they are not fond of it for themselves. Be sure if it offered much they would have a finger—ten of them—in it. When men undertake to sell bustles and hoopskirts, corsets and under-linen to ladies (as they do), holding up the articles for inspection, spreading them about and expatiating on the excellence of the cut, it is not from delicacy, I fancy, that they refrain from the mere stitching of these articles. They do not covet the needle, and they are right. It is the last thing I would turn to; first, because it is so laborious; second, because it is so ill-paid. If it should so happen that I were to lose to-morrow that which I have earned and saved, if people were suddenly to stop coming to my lectures, and publishers were to decline to purchase my *MSS.*; in short, if every resource which I have heretofore employed in earning my livelihood were to be shut off from me, be sure I should not go hire a miserable garret somewhere and try to get some sewing to do; no, verily; I should put myself at my comeliest, wear my cheeriest smile, and stepping from one house to another I should inquire in my choicest vernacular If they wanted a Girl. Does any one want a Girl here? I inquire. Go to! The question is superfluous. They want nothing else but girls. "Girls!" to the Right of us, "Girls!" to the Left of us is cannoned and thundered. Cooks, housemaids, chamber-girls, child's nurses! Hey, ye hundreds of superfluous teachers, ye thousands of ill-paid, under-fed sempstresses, fly to the shelter of warm homes—nice kitchens in which you shall be queen—tidy bedrooms where you may lie snugly and have an extra blanket for the asking—well-kept nurseries with pleasant companionship of the children you tend—these are all awaiting those who seek them. Not a lady of your acquaintance in city or country but has her story to tell about the difficulty of getting good servants.

I grant you there shall be difficulties in your way. I have already indicated some of them. But when and O where, sister woman, do you expect to find a way that shall be without difficulties? I testify that there is no such road in any direction that *I* have traveled.

The only smooth path in this world is the path *downward!*

But then, if you find it an easy thing to drop down from a housetop to the ground below, you are likely to find that the conclusion of your flight will be harder work than any climbing you ever did in your life.

Smooth is the road to ruin, but the end thereof is rough.

6

XII.

MR. TROTMAN sat on our parlor sofa, and I sat on the queer little cane-bottomed chair that Husband bought in one of the Rhine towns—Coblentz, I think. I sat there in front of him, trying to be polite to my guest, but with my blood tingling to hear such pernicious doctrines preached in such a lovely place as our parlor was that morning.

The sun was shining in at the front windows, making every faded bit of red reps glow like woven rubies; the canary was singing such trilling matins as must have reached to heaven; the flowers were growing as if for a race with each other to see which could get ahead in magnificence, and win the most admiring exclamations—the most soulful "Oh's!" every morning from the household; the muslin curtains were as fresh and as prettily done up as a lace handkerchief just from the hands of a French clear-starcher; Algie sat at the piano, picking out a tinkling Sunday-school air in a subdued key with his short fore-finger, but attending to Mr. Trotman, I suspected, with both his little ears wide open; and through it all, through the canary's song and the noise in the street, through the creaking that the little Rhine chair *will* make when you fidget in it, through the rustle of sister Rebecca's form as she moved among the flowers with her watering-pot, through the tinkling of Algie's hymn, Mr. Trotman's unpleasant droning voice sounded self-complacently, as he urged the doctrines of the "liberal" school which he had recently joined.

Oh, the sunniness of that blissful morning! The atmosphere was full of it; the flowers were drinking it; the goldfish splashed in his globe, and borrowed some of it for his coat. Mr. Trotman was in the only shadowy corner of the room; the sunshine did not reach him; and from out the darkness where he sat issued the words which jarred upon me with hideous discord, violating the sweet domesticity of the hour and the scene.

I glanced at Rebecca. Her tall slim figure was draped in her slightly-modified widow's weeds, and her wedding-ring and a mourning ring with her dead Dick's hair, glinted in the sunlight on the third finger of her left hand.

Still she moved about, voiceless, tilting her watering-pot over the flowers, and sometimes stooping to examine a leaf with her careful, intelligent eyes.

Sister Rebecca is the secret of our flowers. She knows them as the scholar his book, the mother her baby. Other people buy gorgeous hot-house plants all in bloom, and pay great prices for them; Rebecca is given an inch or two of cuttings here and there, and when everybody else's flowers are dead, behold hers, flourishing as luxuriantly as cacti in a Louisiana wild!

Such imperturbability—even from her—surprised me a little. I said to myself, "Why is it that I cannot be as cool as our Rebecca is? Here am I just fairly fretting myself into a bad temper, my blood actually engaged in boiling, my teeth in biting my lips angrily; and that cool, unexcitable, and altogether admirable Rebecca is unmoved as a statue, as unfretted as Father Time."

Politeness is second nature to me. It is always easier for me to say an agreeable thing than a disagreeable one. But for once I was tried severely, in my efforts to politely parry

Mr. Trotman's vile blows at everything I love best. The longer he talked, the more the difficulty grew, as, waxing warm in his argument, he waxed bold to the verge of indecency. At last I said,

"Mr. Trotman, you surely do not mean to say that when Mrs. Freelove claims the right to change her husband every day, and that the only restraint on her license should be the limit of her desires, you approve her utterance?"

"Why not?" said he boldly, and with a sudden accession of heat. "I approve everything Mrs. Freelove says," and his eyes flashed. "She believes that marriage trammels the soul of man, and so do I. She believes marriage to be the mother of abominations, and so do I. Abolish marriage and you abolish the social evil. If there were no married men, there would be no fallen women!"

And here occurred that scene which has made so much talk in our circle of acquaintance, and of which such exaggerated accounts have got abroad. Rebecca turned suddenly upon Mr. Trotman, raised her watering-pot and sprinkled him with a little shower of sparkling drops, saying, as she did so, in her cool, unimpassioned way,

"*Get thee behind me, Satan!*"

I thought Mr. Trotman would go through the floor.

How he got out of the house, I scarcely know. I am not sure but he vanished like a stage-imp through a trap-door to an accompaniment of blue fire. He has never called upon us since. I understand he is very bitter in his sarcastic comments upon us, in the choice circle where he is fond of passing his time.

XIII.

THE truth seldom lies at the extremes.

In the matter of marriage, the Mormons and the Free-lovers occupy the extremes—and which is the more abominable it were hard to say.

The Mormon extreme amounts to the tenet that the woman who does not marry will be damned. The Free-love extreme implies that she will be damned if she does marry.

Here, as usual, extremes meet. There is not so much difference between Mormonism and

Free-love as might exist between a black cat and a gray one.

Mrs. Freelove is not married, but lives with a man in the communion of married life. Mrs. Mormon is married to the tenth part of a man, and to that extent she has the advantage in decency of Mrs. Freelove. Yet, between the two there is nothing for an honorable woman to choose. The black cat and the gray cat differ only by a shade.

Neither of these women can ever know the highest bliss this earthly life can give—the bliss of true companionship with a beloved consort. I pity both with all my heart. From what pure delights are they forever shut out!

To soften the (as he calls it) harshness of my judgment regarding Mrs. Freelove, our good-natured but not very long-headed friend Sample said to me recently,

"Well, now, I shouldn't wonder if she preaches worse than she practises. Trotman says so; Trotman knows her intimately. Trotman says that one day he was walking with her all alone in the Central Park, and she said to him in the *sweetest* voice, 'Mr. Trotman, I appreciate how good you are to show yourself in this public place with me. I know how the generality of people regard me. Still, I think they are too hard—I do indeed. Sit down on this bench, and I will tell you something.' And then they sat down on a bench in a quiet place, and she looked right straight in his eyes with her eyes, and then she said, in a voice that he would have taken his Bible oath was truthful, 'Mr. Trotman, as true as I live, I never'"——

Here Mr. Sample suddenly blushed violently, and stammered out "'pon my word, though, I didn't think how confounded immodest that was in her, till now when I've undertaken to tell the story in the presence of ladies."

Wretched woman! to be so lost to modesty that she has no shame in a conversation of this sort, between herself and a young married man, on a bench in a quiet place in Central Park! It was a scene which I will match for you in the first French novel we pick up. Heroines of French novels—held up to the execration of virtuous people all over the world—are constantly indulging in this sort of scene. Time and place are exactly fitting. The beautiful park—the seclusion in the midst of a crowd, birds twittering their love-songs overhead, leaves bursting with warmth and gladness, the soft winds wooing—the rich equipages passing at a distance, the voice subdued to a tone of flattering confidence—

Get thee behind me, Satan! The trail of the serpent is there ; we know its slime ; you cannot persuade us it is healthy moisture—dew, for instance, or vivifying rain from heaven.

And be sure that I who write you these lines do so with a full knowledge of how terrible a blade is calumny. I have seen good women stabbed to the heart by it, thrown over into the black waters of the river of Despair by it; I have seen loving hearts sundered by it, loyal confidence destroyed by it ; households broken up by it, the fair sun in Heaven clouded for tear-blinded eyes by it. "Give me but an atom of truth for a basis," said a lady witness in a St. Louis court-room recently, "and I will ruin the character of any woman in the world."

It is the entirely thoughtless, or the entirely vicious only, who really make a business of calumniating. I am as afraid of injuring a woman's character by injudicious comment as I am of handling a kerosene lamp or a bottle of oxalic acid. I am afraid of hurting myself as well as the other person. You cannot keep clean hands when you dabble in the mud. I like my hands to be clean. But you will remember that it was neither you nor I, reader, who went after Mrs. Freelove, looked in her house and found two husbands there. She herself came forth, introduced her husbands, held up for imitation a plurality of husbands, urged young girls to take any number of husbands, called upon the law to sanction any mad animalism any sensualist's brain could devise. It is not what others have said of her, but what she has said of herself, that excites the disgust and reprobation of every Christian man and woman in this and other lands. What she has done, is between her and God; He shall judge her for that; but what she has said might pervert the morals of our little Algie, and God allows me to judge her for that; and if this book proved but a shield for that one—or any other one—young heart, it were worth the writing.

Before I saw Mrs. Freelove and her Sister I had heard that they were women who had been engaged in telling fortunes to men in dingy rooms in Western towns, and the general impression was that their own fortunes were as dubious as those they "told"—their characters as dingy as their rooms. Knowing how cheap is this sort of condemnation of women who feel that the washtub and the sewing-machine are not their vocation, and that these are already overcrowded with votaries, I paid no more heed to these warnings than if they had not been uttered.

"It seems too bad folks *will* be so hateful," said a sweet girl of nineteen to me the other day in New Orleans; "Amanda L. went and got a place in the Dollar Store—the only store she could get in, as they don't have girl clerks in stores here in New Orleans, except in the French quarter. She gets seven dollars a week, and since she's been there everybody has cut her—they say it's not respectable to stand in a Dollar Store, and that she's lost her reputation. Even the other Sunday-school teachers are cool to her. She says, All right; she won't go to church and Sunday-school any more. Church and Sunday-school won't feed her, and seven dollars a week will."

It would be interesting to learn whether a lovely young girl who had really lost her reputation could not make more than seven dollars a week out of what remained to her as that lost reputation's equivalent, and not be obliged to stand on her feet from eight o'clock in the morning till ten at night in a Dollar Store.

If a woman tells me she is chaste I will believe her. She is the only person who should know. So fond are men of trifling with the good name of women that I will accept no man's testimony as against her own.

But, what do I care how chaste she be, if she gets up and preaches the doctrine of unchastity?

The only time I remember hearing my father rebuke my mother—it was a gentle rebuke, more in sorrow than in anger—was on one occasion when, on hearing of the glittering success of some wicked person of their acquaintance, she made one of those remarks which rise to the lips of almost every one, at some time or another, that Vice seemed always to triumph, and Virtue was often a discouraging business. He told her that he knew well enough she did not mean what she said, and that she would be the last person to gain fortune or position at sacrifice of the very smallest of those beautiful qualities which made her so precious to us all—

but, that it would be wise to avoid such injudicious and unmeant remarks as this one, for there were young children about, who would remember what she said. And to show that he was right, here am I remembering it, though I am sure I was not more than ten years old when the circumstance happened, and no one has ever referred to it since.

And I remembered the answer, too! And I remember that mother fully agreed with its judgment, and reproached herself for her thoughtlessness. Dear father—long in your grave, where soon we all shall lie:—dear mother,—yet by God's blessing spared to us,—your children love you and bless you, and thank you for all your counsels, which have stood them in good stead in many a weary strife.

Not all the tortures of the inquisition should make me point the finger of scorn at any living woman, and charge her with being unchaste, a free-lover, in face of her denial. But a woman stands forth before the world and says,

"I am a free-lover! I believe it is my right to change my husband daily, if I wish. I believe that a woman should boldly and openly live as wife with a man to whom she is not married. I live with two men, one of whom is my present consort, the other my discarded consort, and I am not married to either of them."

I think with regard to this person it may be said that Calumny's occupation's gone.

When an egg advertises its own rottenness, in that language with which it is endowed, it is not necessary for any bystander to explain wherein it is rotten, or assay the quality of its rottenness.

I do not go any further than Mrs. Freelove's own public utterances in dealing with the subject—it is not needful.

There are certain good women who associate with Mrs. Freelove, and welcome what they deem her aid to the woman-suffrage cause—not perceiving that she is killing it, for the present generation at least. And because these good women associate with her, certain lookers-on argue that Mrs. Freelove is good also—or Mrs. Standfirm would not tolerate her.

Hark ye, friends—have ye all forgotten Mrs. Standfirm's speech in the Woman's Suffrage Convention of 186—, when she said, defending George Prancer Brain, these words?

"Call Mr. Brain a lunatic if you will. He has

helped us nobly. If the devil himself were to come to me and say 'Mrs. Standfirm, let me aid you,' I would reply, 'Thank you Mr. Devil, your aid is very welcome.'"

If you remember that, as I do (and I believe that the utterance is yet to be found in print with Mrs. Standfirm's name to it) I hope you will not again cite Mrs. Standfirm's good moral character (undoubted, to be sure) as a warrant for that of Mrs. Freelove. Mrs. Standfirm has given the promised welcome to Satan, that's all, instead of bidding him "Get thee behind me!"

XIV.

THE two women who have made themselves principally notorious in connection with free love, I met, in the first days of their coming before the public. They were then merely women who had opened a new field of business operation for woman. In such a motion as that, every woman who has the welfare of her sex at heart supported them. I did, most cordially. They said they were experts at financiering. For myself I know as much about financiering as about engineering, but if they had said they had talent for the latter instead of the former I should have heartily responded "Amen! Clear the track! God be with you!" They were extremely non-committal in regard to any stand for woman more decided than that which they themselves had at that time taken; were not so sure that the ballot was desirable, or woman-suffrage feasible. Nothing was said in regard to marriage, and I supposed they were what they seemed; one an honest married woman, the other an honest unmarried girl. My heart is fond to weakness of young girls, and this one even in a short interview awakened my interest, and my tenderness. Daintily tricked in girlish prettiness, she was to my blinded vision pure, sweet, and lovable; I looked in her eyes and shook her hand, and wished her well. That she was chaste I took for granted. Can you not easily understand how she fell from her pedestal of purity, rolled in the mud besmeared with foulness, when I discovered that by her own avowal she was a free lover?—"not necessarily an incontinent," as one of her apologists explained, "but most decidedly a free lover!"

A person living in absolute iniquity, who yet

extols virtue and execrates vice, is less a blight to the community than one who lives chastely but preaches vice. In the first instance it is only his own soul he is damning; in the second he is trying and perhaps succeeding in damning the souls of other people. It is this which nullifies the complaint of free-love women that their private lives, which are their private business, are judged by persons who are no more moral than themselves, and that these hypocritically denounce them when they are themselves no better. It is certainly true that he who casts the first stone should be sinless; but even a sinful person (and who is not a sinful person?) may rebel with an indignation worthy of an angel against teaching young souls that vice is virtue.

A man has sinned—a woman has sinned—but they *know* they have sinned. They are perhaps sorry for it. Their daily effort is to subdue the evil propensities of nature—to go and sin no more.

An argument which the Mormons consider especially strong in support of their position is that it ill behooves Gentiles to be horrified at plurality of wives while marital infidelity is rampant among them, outside of Utah. It needs the fury of fanatics to make out such a case as this; with a profound appreciation of the moral failings of our men, I am yet fully convinced that this infidelity is comparatively a rare sin among them. Thank God the great bulk of the men of this country are Christians who know and believe that the Seventh Commandment was meant for both men and women.

But even those who transgress know well enough that they *are* transgressing. The poor-rich adventurer whose life of wild iniquity was finished by his rival's bullet, knew well enough that his life *was* iniquitous. He knew he was sinning. He asked and obtained the forgiveness of the sweet woman who loved him and bore his name. And asking her forgiveness was but a roundabout way of asking for that of God. Perhaps he even asked that of God. Who knows what may have been the remorseful pains which shook his soul in moments of seclusion?

But even he—who set social laws at defiance—did not presume to say that his path was the right path. On the contrary, I remember a speech he made which struck me so forcibly that I am able at this remote hour to give the substance of what he said as it lingers in my memory. He was addressing some of the discontented ones among his railway employés, and he said in effect:

"Boys, it may strike you as a fine thing to wear a velvet coat, and a diamond pin, and lavender-colored kids; but, believe me, under that coat there may be a heart which don't know what such a thing as peace or happiness is. And I tell you if such a man did not get into a sort of whirlpool which swings him around so he can't free himself from it, he would gladly be like one of you, earning honest wages which he takes home to a good wife and loving children at the end of the week, and smoking his pipe with a free conscience and in comfort. It might very well be that, instead of you envying me, it would be more fit for me to envy you. But a man gets going in a certain way, and people envy him, when the fact is he's leading *a hell of a life!*"

Even this poor moralist—whose practices were notoriously bad, and whose teachings of any kind were few—did not attempt to palliate his wickedness by asserting that the hell of a life which he lived, was a heaven of a life, which humanity at large would do well to emulate.

The worst effect of the spread of free-love doctrines would be, the destruction of the only mundane world that is entirely pure, the only gold in which there is no dross, the only diamond in which there is no flaw. I mean of course that world of beauty, purity, domestic bliss, peace, content, everything true hearts love best—that central point around which circles the best that there is in our civilization—and which is all enwrapt in that little word, Home.

I read in the newspapers that Mrs. Freelove owns a beautiful house in a pleasant quarter of the city of New York. Here is the thing for which the worthiest of the great mass of people are struggling—the possession of a *home*—the ownership of a house under whose blessed and protecting roof-tree all of their clan may gather—where friends may come to visit—where that angel of God intrusted with the lending of baby souls to mortals may enter when he will—where that other angel of God intrusted with the glorious work of wafting them back to Heaven must enter when he must. All this is hallowed. Those bricks, that mortar, those plumber's pipes, that carpenter-work, are not merely bricks, mortar, lead and wood—they are the toiler's epic poem, his every-day church, his shrine by the wayside. A tortoise and a snail have their homes ready made; you and the birds make yours. And when you have made it well, and keep it sweet with love, clean with noble tending, large enough for all good impulses, too small for free-love and other kindred deviltries, it merits whatever of affection you lavish in or on it. No fear of pagan idolatry, of mere materiality in almost worshipping such a home as this; it is the spirit which dwells there which you reverence. Paper made of rags of untold filth, ink ill-smelling, black and vile, yon imp whistling "Tommy Dodd" as he sets each stickful, tell me the story of the Ser mon on the Mount. Christ shines up from that printed, material page with an effulgence that dazzles; and His very spirit clears away the grossness which might linger in the love you bear the building-lot where stands your home.

Let us see how this thing we call home is esteemed by Mrs. Freelove. We violate no sanctity of privacy in crossing this threshold;

we have the testimony of the newspaper reporters who have called there for this part of the story.

A body of men—mostly strangers to the women they are about to visit—go to the house on Sunday night. They pull the bell, and the door is opened by Mrs. Freelove's youngest sister—a free-lover to the core, also.

"Come in," she cries, in hearty fashion, "Come right in, all of you. Walk into the parlor. It's all right. *This is just like a political club!*"

And into this Sunday-night female "political club" these strange men enter, to find a crowd of other men and a few women, talking excitedly on free-love, woman-suffrage, female presidency, and like appropriate Sabbath-day topics. The room is just what we should have expected it to be; it is lined with big mirrors, and a great deal of gas is burning and the principal furniture is chairs and sofas to accommodate sitters.

We at home who sit cosily around our five-dollar second-hand Table at breakfast and read the account in the newspapers on Monday morning, say to each other,

"What a home!"

XV.

APROPOS of this gaudy home (if it be not wicked to call it by a name so dear), the conversation turned on mirrors.

"Do you not think that Americans pay too much deference to the mirror as an object of decoration?"

"Yes," said I, "a mirror is a French importation which ought to be used sparingly. One touch too much of mirror makes the whole world a saloon."

Give me some white and gold, some red satin and plenty of mirrors and I will turn you out a bar-room-like parlor enough to freeze your blood.

I grant you that these ingredients are seductive to the general run of housekeepers; but I have tested them and know how unsatisfactory they are. At one period of my life I lived in such a parlor as this. I do not mean I occupied it in a lodging-house. I mean I was supposed to be the mistress of it. Do not ask me how supposed. That would open up a history which is too long to be printed in these pages, and which will perhaps see the light somewhere else. Suffice it to say that this place was my home. An upholsterer furnished it from the hanging of the pictures to the placing of the shovel and tongs. Not one small atom of soul was in the rich furniture and the soft velvet carpets; no tinge of heart gleamed through the folds of the expensive lace curtains. People would come in and sit down; and at first they would say, "How handsome your parlors are!" but somehow they didn't seem to make themselves right comfortable there. No woman ever brought out her knitting and spent the afternoon; no man ever lounged cosily, peacefully reading a newspaper or a magazine. Full of expensive *fauteuils*, there wasn't an easy chair in the room.

It seemed to me as if myself and everybody else came at length to partake of the qualities of the furniture. Human legs turned into mahogany like the chairs; human forms were clothed in red satin lambrequins like the window curtains; human eyes were polished French looking-glass; human cheeks were ghastly white moulding; human lips were gilt and fresco.

All over this great country such parlors are

to be seen. Here in New York there are hundreds and hundreds of them. You know what a good story Rebecca tells about her visit to her old schoolmate, Harriet B. Harriet had been recently married—(six weeks before she was married her beau called to take her driving to Central Park; she flung down his card and stamped on it, and made faces in the direction of the parlor where he was sitting; then she cried out "*Darn* him! I'd rather pull his hair than go!")—um—um—where was I? Oh, to be sure! She struck this good match on her flinty heart, and he became a flame. So they were married, and had recently moved into a grand new house in Madison Square. Hatty was famously stuck up about the satin furniture, and the pier-glasses between the windows, and the big square mirrors over the mantelpieces, and her Steinway Grand (Hatty can play "The Campbells are Coming" pretty well, except that she makes mistakes in the bass), and she was very anxious to show Rebecca what she had got in return for suppressing her desire to pull hair. So, one afternoon, Rebecca called and was ushered into the satin parlor, and—very naturally—she sat down.

Harriet flew down stairs to meet her, dressed in a not over-clean wrapper, but then she said she didn't want to keep Rebecca waiting, which was kind. They kissed, and Rebecca's heart swelled with pleasure to see that Hatty was so comfortably—or rather magnificently, housed; for our blessed Rebecca has a heart as big as a mountain, and she loves Hatty with all her faults. Being tired she sat down again, having risen to greet Hatty when she came in.

But strange to say, Hatty didn't sit down; she stood up most awkwardly, and bent over Rebecca sitting there, and rattled on about the no-end of fine things she'd got—clothes at the dressmaker's, and three new hats, and a promise of a Cashmere shawl from her husband, and a porcelain dinner-service, and ever so much fine linen. But all the time she seemed so fidgety, Rebecca didn't know what to make of it.

Finally she jerked Rebecca's arm, and said "Becky, come look out of the window; I want to show you something."

But there wasn't anything special to see, and when they turned to sit down again, Hatty took Rebecca's arm, and chattering innocently the while, walked her over to where two wicker chairs were standing, and almost pushed her into one, and took the other herself.

"It was as plain as the nose on my face," says Rebecca—and mercy knows that's plain enough—"that she was restless because I was sitting on one of the satin chairs, and that's the reason she didn't sit down herself. Those chairs are to be looked at, not to be sat down upon."

Hatty is another type of American woman curious enough to contemplate. She is an almost ideally good housekeeper; and sew! oh, how her fingers do fly over the material! and she's as neat as she is rapid. She says she won't ever buy a sewing-machine, nasty, botchy, and expensive things. She can sew fast enough for her purposes, and likes her dresses made every stitch "just so." And she bakes pies, and roasts, and cleans and dusts, and rubs the brasses till you can see your face in them. She can't keep a servant long; not one of them is up to her standard of excellence. She has paid for that satin furniture long ago, by scrimping in the kitchen. Her husband dines down town, and she eats bread and cheese or cold meat at home.

Her husband is worth only about three hundred thousand dollars, and they are anxious to get a little money together for their old age.

You'd never suspect these things when you were looking at the house from the outside, or contemplating the satin furniture and pier-glasses from within, or meeting Hatty herself dressed in a magnificent silk walking-suit with frills and puffs and velvet headings and thread-lace edgings innumerable. You'd think that costume came from Paris. Oh no—Hatty would be horrified at the idea of wasting her poor husband's money in that way. She bought the paper pattern for twenty-five cents, ransacked every shop in New York, not to mention Brooklyn, to get the material at its lowest; then cut and basted and fitted and finished it to the last hook and eye herself.

Judging from the European standpoint, and looking at this elegant house from the opposite side of the way, and perhaps seeing Hatty herself coming down the steps dressed in her best, you would say, "This is the abode of an aristocrat—well, let us say a merchant prince—that is his lady consort; the house is full of servants, male and female, and dinners are given there noted for reckless profusion, rich wines and dainty dishes, thrice a week."

But if you could peer in through the roof and see Hatty in her loose and unbecoming wrapper, munching bread and cheese, or jerking old friends off her satin chairs and planting them down on rickety wicker ones, you would perhaps say "So ho! Mr. and Mrs. Sham live here."

I shall not soon forget the remark of a young Englishman newly arrived who was walking along Michigan Avenue in Chicago one day long before the fire. He gazed admiringly at the handsome residences, and pointing to one which was rather more noticeably gorgeous than the others, he said to his friend with a sigh, "I suppose if you or I had but the silver plate which is in that house, it would make us rich for life."

He would have been surprised indeed to learn that there wasn't a silver spoon in the house, and that the master thereof was at that moment blacking his own boots, while his good wife was engaged in making the beds. Neither of these occupations is in the least degrading; but being ashamed of them is.

The Englishman's observation was based on

that wide-spread and excellent English custom which ordains that no man should (because it is unsafe) spend more than one-fifth part of his income for house-rent. But these Chicago people, in common with a certain number of people all over the country, were living in a house with such an expensive rent that every quarter-day they were half-distracted how to scrape together enough to pay the landlord.

Oh, what a miserable soul-grinding existence! Oh, what a price to pay for the shabby sham of living behind a worse than grave-stone front!

You will be very much mistaken if you suppose that I do not believe in economy at home. I do. I believe in make-shifts even, when they are not calculated to degrade the character of the make-shifter. If Hatty had married a poor man, all those traits in her which now seem contemptible would become virtues. Having married a rich man, and having assumed before the world to keep up the style of a fashionable lady in an elegant home, I don't admire her bread-and-cheese ways or her little tuppenny tricks one bit.

If I had a husband with three hundred thousand dollars (and I beg you not to believe that I want anything of the sort), if I had such a husband as Hatty's, and such a home, I would show my consort what money was good for. Instead of eating bread-and-cheese alone, I would have my friends to dinner, and give them a good dinner, every day in the week. Instead of spending my time chasing from shop to shop to get a yard of two-penny tape for one penny, I would buy books and read them, songs and sing them, pictures and enjoy them; and in every way I could, I would make my home a joy to every soul that came near it, even to the professional beggar-woman who makes her everlasting fortune going from basement door to door with a basket on her arm, and woe in her eyes—and who long ago learned the futility of rapping at Hatty's area-gate, you may be sure. Hatty hates beggars worse than Betsy Trotwood hated donkeys, and drives them off with much the same frantic indignation.

As my lot now is, I wear my turned black silks with a light heart, and thank Heaven that by economies such as this and others equally legitimate we have been able to get a home which I love far better than I should ever love Hatty's.

I know a woman whose husband had, in the early days of their marriage, but one white duck suit; and it was in fact the only suit he owned which was not too heavy to wear during a long, hot summer. Now this nobly-proud woman washed, starched, and ironed that one duck suit every single night, the whole summer long, and sent hubbie out to his business fresh as a rose every morning. She made no sham pretenses in the market-place in respect to the large number of white duck suits her husband possessed; probably no one ever noticed or thought anything about it except to see how sweetly fresh and clean Neighbor Jones always managed to keep; but I tell you that it is these little acts—of goodness or the reverse—which make up our lives and by which we shall be judged; and I firmly believe that the steam of those nightly soapsuds mounted as high as heaven; and that for the diurnal washing, starching, and ironing of that white duck suit, Neighbor Jones's wife stands accredited—under the equivalent heads of wifely pride, womanly devotion, and beautiful marital love—with a thousand golden merit-marks on the book of the recording angel.

XVI.

SOMETIMES people say to me "The truth is, I am obliged to keep up an appearance. It would hurt me in my business if people were to think I am not well off. I must make a show."

It was this logic (not mine, but that of another party, and I was overborne) which took me into that ghastly, bemirrored, red satin and gilt moulding drawing-room I told you of just now. And the moral of the story would be lost if I failed to mention that it was exactly this move —of seeming to be in possession of means which he had not—which lost my logician the game. He befooled everybody so well, that he befooled the people who employed him. They, seeing the style he was living in, imagined he must be robbing them, and so discharged him.

A man who has passed years in a community has lived an arid life indeed, if his worth and excellence have not penetrated further than his own household, and given him a standing among his townsmen which money can neither add to, nor take from. I should like to know if Henry Ward Beecher is valued by his community on account of his income? Or is it on account of the nourishing food for mind and heart which he lavishes for all men and women who can read, and for the few thousands who can get near him to hear? Is Robert Collyer thought much of in Chicago for any style in which he lives, any parties he gives? Or is it for the beauty which he throws into the life which now is, for all who come in contact with him?

I could name lawyers, doctors, merchants who wield a similar though smaller influence. No one cares whether they are wealthy or not.

But if you can afford to live in fine style, and if you can lead a better and nobler life in a grand mansion than you can in a modest one—if you can even do better work there, why then there is no reason whatever—social, moral, or religious—why you should not go and live there.

Sometimes we make great mistakes in these expectations, however. I knew an American lady whose contributions to the English press were universally admired about ten years ago. Many of her choicest effusions were written on the kitchen table; her thoughts on the manuscript, her eyes on the chops. Sometimes the soup would boil over while she was in the middle of a word, and she had to drop the pen and fly to remove the pot-lid. Time and steam wait for no authoress. Also, children have little respect for the great thoughts which move in the brain of the mamma who, they know from experience, can't keep a nurse-girl. Hence the frequent interruptions from little tongues which urged "bread and butter!" — "so sleepy!" — "drink o' water!" — "tell me story!"—"take me walkin'!"—"Johnnie bit me!"—"me got tummach-ache!"

"Never mind," she would say to me, "one of these days I shall have an elegant study, all to myself; quiet; the children out walking with a good, kind nurse; a beautiful study hung with rich, scholarly, sombre blue velvet—with a carved oak desk—and a leathern chair which revolves—and a marble bust of Pallas just above my chamber door. Then shall I bring forth work! true poetry, rich humor, sparkling wit that outbubbles the wine on the Rhine. You shall see! only wait."

We waited. Not exactly for that transforma

tion which seemed as likely to happen as that Aladdin himself should appear, and bring her a blue velvet study and a kind nurse and put a marble bust of Pallas just above her chamber door; but because—unless we committed suicide—we could not do otherwise than wait.

And will you believe it? Almost before we knew it, See-saw, whose poverty-weighted end had been tipped to the very ground for years with this poor woman on it, sprang suddenly into the air and landed her high and dry in the blue velvet study!

Not a detail lacking; the good, kind nurse, the pacified children, the leathern revolving chair, the marble bust of Pallas just above her chamber door.

And the work—the true poetry, the rich humor, the sparkling wit that outbubbles the wine of the Rhine?

Absent from the roll-call!

She never knew how it was, but what she did principally in the revolving chair was to revolve; the blue velvet seemed to fold about her and smother inspiration; Pallas hadn't an idea in her marble head; more than once in despair she rushed into the nursery, scrubbed the children's faces, darned their socks, and gave the nurse a half holiday.

"Too much is expected of me now," she said; "the oaken desk would feel itself insulted if I produced no finer things on it than those I brought off the kitchen table. Crushed by this fear, I produce nothing. Then, too, the room itself is a constant reproach. It seems to say 'Here am I, madam, an excellent room, well lighted, heated, dry, airy and well-furnished—a room which numbers of persons as refined, as well-educated, as worthy as yourself would gratefully receive, and ask no better housing all the rest of their lives; and you forsooth come here lackadaisically every day, and twist yourself on my son that revolving chair, or stare impertinently in the face of my daughter Miss Pallas, and yet do nothing further than this toward producing a masterpiece. Come now!—at once produce a masterpiece!'"

The rest goes without saying—*cela va sans dire.* She wrote no more. Her literary ability became a remembrance only—a once upon a time—a long, long ago!

And does it follow from this that the sacred fire keeps best alight near the kitchen stove, and the divine afflatus needs "Gim'me piece bread and butter!" from baby lips to win it to life?

That depends.

But one thing is clearly proven; and that is that a blue velvet study won't write your new book for you.

—By the way (though this has nothing to do with the subject), isn't it curious what different influences affect different writers? W., when he wishes to write, takes down a volume of Emerson's Essays and tones himself up with them, until he gets so fully into the Emersonian spirit that he feels like another Emerson himself —or feels that he would like to be. His mind pitched—like instruments at the opera—to the highest intellectual key, he sits down and produces something better than he would otherwise have done. Aim at the Bishop's gown, you'll get one of the sleeves. But for me, oh dear no, thank you; when I have anything to write I prefer not to attack such an intellectual eminence as Emerson. He crushes me. It is as if Paganini were to get up before a young violinist and play for an hour or two at his grandest; then say, "Come now, let's see what you can do." What would be the effect of this? Would it not be to discourage the young man? Would he not be likely to say, "Oh dear no, there's no use trying. If violin-playing has been carried with the aid of grand genius to such perfection as that, there's no use my hoping to succeed. I'll give up."

I can only write by remembering that I've got something to say—must say it. As for literary quality, no matter—my audience will get my meaning into their heads if I only aim at their hearts. So I write—from the heart to the heart; and I am encouraged in doing this by finding that I have at least as large an audience as Emerson has; not intellectual prodigies, perhaps (as his readers are, of course)—but such as they are, God made them.

XVII.

WE have been housekeeping about a year.

It is not pride of ownership that makes me say we have a beautiful house; and when I say beautiful, I refer to the beauty which comes from comfort, from desirable "improvements,"

improvements which really improve; not from an imposing frontal, nor a mansard roof. Yet there is gas in every room, the kitchen by no means excepted, hot and cold running water all over the house, stationary washtubs, great closets, large enough to serve on a pinch as bedrooms, and other snug household comforts such as servants delight in.

For a week or two we got along with no other servant than a charwoman—not that she called herself by this, or any other convenient name. She was Mis Cox, a married woman, charged a dollar and a half a day and her board, came late, went early, ate tremendously, worked the reverse. We soon saw that we must have a permanent girl; for Mis Cox numbered among her other eccentricities a habit of not coming at all, some days, leaving us in grave astonishment and breathless breakfastlessness.

Sister Rebecca put on her bonnet and went to what Mis Cox called the Intelligent office. What happened when she got there I know not; but this is certain: when she came home the cupboard was bare and so the poor dog (and people) had none (i.e. no food, for I feel that I must explain this).

Eureka! She has found her! Treasure trove! a girl!

She happened to be a middle-aged woman, Irish, sulky. If she had been a wild horse of the Pampas, and Rebecca had lassoed her and dragged her to our corral with the rope hanging around her neck, she could not have looked more restive and discontented. We agreed to pay her fifteen dollars a month wages and get a second girl to help her as soon as possible. And we took her without a recommendation. We thought it unwise to ask her for it, fearing she would take offense and go away without getting us our dinner. Rebecca was quite capable of getting it for us; but through Mis Cox's defections she had got dinners and washed dishes till she was tired out.

"Be plased to show me over the house, Mim," said our Acquisition.

On timid inquiry we found our Acquisition's name to be Bridget. Yes, she was the celebrated Bridget we had so often read about.

Rebecca showed her over the house, into every room, every nook, every cranny. It is just possible that in her pride at our newly-bought house, Rebecca may have expected that there would fall some words of commendation from the lips of Bridget. If so, she was disappointed. Not a sound was heard, not a funeral note.

At length Rebecca said: "You see there is everything of the most convenient character, water, gas, &c. We have just moved in, and things are of course unsettled; but the carpets are all down, and anything that is too heavy for you to do we shall have done by a man. This is your room."

A bright, cheerful little third-story back, with a clean bed, and a large soft rug on the floor, and abundant shelves, and even a bottle of holy water—left there by Mis Cox.

Mutism continued on the part of Bridget.

Nothing more remaining to be shown this fastidious person, they descended to the kitchen. Rebecca began giving her instructions for dinner.

"You will boil this rice, please, Bridget, and bake those potatoes; and—"

"Ye nadent tell me fwat to do, Mim; I'm not going to shtop, Mim; the place don't shoot me, Mim."

"Oh, very well," said our marvellously cool

sister (Vesuvius was nothing to *me*, when I heard this), "but don't think of going till after dinner. You'll be hungry."

The ruse succeeded. After dinner was over, Bridget slung on her shawl, banged the basement door, and left us alone in our glory.

Now for the sum of one dollar Rebecca had purchased the right to draw blank girls out of the Intelligent office lottery for the space of one month, by which time she was supposed to have drawn her prize; if not, she could gamble in servant-girls for another month, and another, and so on till chaos comes again, or her dollars give out. But fancy the uninviting prospect of marching in a procession of Bridgets at the front door, only to see them march themselves out at the basement ditto!

Once again Rebecca's fairy-like form confronted the monarch of the Intelligent office. He was surprised that that girl should have acted so. She was a splendid girl—truly sp—lendid! Unfortunately there was not another girl in the place.

This was discouraging.

But he had others elsewhere; oh, yes. His resources were limitless. He had a French girl—at home now with her husband, but he would send a note to her, she would gladly come—a superb cook! Did we like French cookery? Should think we did? All right, then. The only trouble was that she was just over from France and didn't speak a word of English. Oh, we had a lady in the house who could speak French! That was fortunate. Now, if by any chance she should be already engaged, he had a German girl, excellent girl, but she only spoke German. Never mind, we had a gentleman in the house who spoke German. Then there was no longer any fear of our not getting *somebody*.

Rebecca was growing desperate. She told him to send us a girl, no matter what her nationality. O. spoke French, and W. spoke German, and Algie talked Hog Latin like a native hog; and if necessary, the first two would leave their business, and Algie would stay home from school, and the whole three of us would go sit in a row in the kitchen and devote our entire time and energies to translating the housekeeper's orders to the cook.

By showing such an accommodating spirit as this, the Intelligent man became convinced, that, though it was not for mortals to command success, we certainly deserved it. He politely begged Rebecca to go home now, and before long the coveted girl would surely be forthcoming.

At the end of twenty-four hours, she forthcame.

Would you believe it, she was—

But why should I ask Would you believe it? Of course you will believe it. You will find it not at all difficult to believe. Such persons are not rare. They may be counted by millions. But then to us it was such a surprise. Because the man had not hinted at such a thing, and there was not the slightest indication of his office transacting business for these people. She was Black.

Oh, but Black—even with a capital letter—is no word for her. She was a chimney-pot—she was a black marble statue on a black marble monument on a moonless, starless night. She was hot, too, as well as black, and in perspiring exuded ink.

Our geraniums thrive like weeds, and their sweet odor fills all the air; but it was hot, and Sarah Hoggins perspired ink, and the flower-pots arose as one man, presented her the hilt of their perfumed sword, and avowed themselves vanquished.

She held out a torn slip of very dirty pink paper, and though it was greasy — perhaps having been used on some occasion to wrap a quarter pound of butter in—we managed to decipher the glad tidings that this was Sarah Hoggins, and she had Been living with Me 7 mons. She had always found Her Honnest. If anybody wanted a Honnest woman they would Do well to engage Sarah for she had found Her to be Honnest. Mrs. T. Jones.

We retired into an adjoining room to lay our heads together. The result was: an extraordinary unanimity of feeling against employing a black woman. Fully recognizing the undoubted merits of hundreds and hundreds of clean, intelligent and worthy black women, we also recognized the extreme doubtfulness of Sarah Hoggins belonging to this class.

Besides, Rebecca's mother (our mothers, though far away, were still our guiding stars) had never employed a colored person; mine had, and didn't like her. Algie's argument was couched in excellent hog-English (he wields a good knife and fork, the boy does): "You couldn't tell whether her hands were clean or dirty when she was kneading the pie-crust." W.'s was powerful and unanswerable: "She smells bad."

"Now look here," said Rebecca, "let us be reasonable."

We immediately proceed to be reasonable.

"Do we or do we not want a girl?"

"We do, we do!" chorus of Slaves.

"Then let us take this one."

"She's black!"

"What of it? I'm tired out. I'd take her if she was green."

"Perhaps she is—green and black, too."

"No repartee allowed, because I haven't time to think what to say back," says Rebecca. "I concede the undeniable fact that Sarah is a colored person."

"Colored! She's blacker than the ace of spades!" growls Algie.

"Well, friends, again I ask, what of it? Why, good gracious!" and our quiet Rebecca lifted her hands deprecatingly, "this is growing political! Can it be that this dining-room is an amateur Senate? Is the old prejudice against color again springing up? Are we Southern Oligarchs — Dixian aristocrats — pecunious Conservatives?"

We regretfully reply that we are not. We are people with a big Wash on hand, and three meals a day to get, and we want a girl.

"Then take Hoggins. Let the bells go ringing for Sarah."

To this we finally agree. Whatever else she may be, it appears Sarah Hoggins is honest. Mrs. T. Jones asserts it. Who Mrs. T. Jones is we know not, and have no means of knowing. But we want an honest girl. We do not desire that our watches shall be stolen nor our pockets picked. Honesty is the best policy! It is our best policy to take honesty and Sarah.

Our minds fully made up, we march in to the culprit. She seems far less concerned than we are, and is adjusting her boot-lace with a more extended display of dirty stocking than is pleasing to an æsthetic taste.

She is certainly a grotesque figure, as she stands up to receive our decision. She is exactly the negro wench of the Minstrel stage. She wears an immense woolly, wobbly waterfall, and an absurd little hat garnished with red and yellow flowers, pulled down over her eyes and resting on her fat greasy nose. Her dress sticks up behind, and shows the heels of her worn-out boots. Her shawl is a flame—subdued by dirt—of yellow and red. Her fingers are covered with brass rings. She takes back Mrs. T. Jones's valuable contribution to literature, and opening her dress she sticks it into her bosom. We now understand why the pink paper was greasy.

She grumbles at our fifteen dollars a month, says she has always had sixteen, and before we can answer says All right, she'll take it. Then we tell her that we want her to get at the washing immediately; at which she looks surprised, as if it were quite strange that people should have washing. To be sure, *she* can't have much.

She goes upstairs to prepare herself, and when she comes down she is so altered that we think it must be another woman. The waterfall has gone off her head, and all her gorgeous rigging has vanished; leaving her bare poles—to speak nautically—enshrouded in a light and dirty calico wrapper, cut bias, loose at the waist, and trailing in rags behind her on the ground. She immediately asks for a bottle of oxalic acid.

Perhaps you think we were surprised at this. I was; but Rebecca to my astonishment went and produced what she asked for, as complacently as if it were the vinegar-cruet.

"She wants it to clean the boiler," said Rebecca.

But as she never did clean the boiler, this was a mistake. She kept that bottle three days and I was in agony the whole time.

I frankly confess here and now, that there are two things I am afraid of: one is a kerosene lamp, the other is a bottle of oxalic acid. The first I expect to explode every moment; the second I expect to up and pour itself down our stomachs and kill us whether we will or no.

When Sarah returned it, the bottle was empty.

Rebecca's theory was that she must have poured it into the boiler-full of clothes. Everything was faded, torn, lay around wet for a week, and became hopelessly mildewed.

Sarah soon developed an unsuspected ability for heavy profanity, and for falling to sleep every time she sat down. As she sat down pretty constantly, her slumbers were frequent. We bore it all as long as we could. Then we told her she must go. She was furious. She said that she would be profaned if she'd gwo without a monf's pay; she wuz a po' culled guhl an'd been a slabe all her days, an' now she had come Norf she'd be profaned if she'd gwo 'out her money.

Algie here remarked to her that she'd better go before his father came home, or she'd be arrested for bad language.

To this Sarah replied that as for dat profane sassy boy she'd knock his excessively profane head off if he didn't hold his sassy tongue.

Here W. *did* come in, and asked, man-fashion, "What's all this?"

Sarah became as meek as a lamb, and went off up-stairs for her bundle.

While she was gone Algie told the story of Sarah's remarks, and when W. went to pay her he said,

"I'm sorry you should think it necessary to swear, Sarah. That won't do at all. You must unlearn that, if you are going to live in respectable families."

"Fo' de Lord, boss," said Sarah, with

eyes as big as saucers, "I nevah cussed a dam."

Sarah left her bundle in the basement hall while she went looking for another place, and privately informed Algie, who turned the door-key on her, that if we stole anything out of it while she was gone she'd have us all up befo' de jedge.

Whereupon Rebecca untied her bundle at once, and searched it carefully for spoons. But there were none. We had watched her too closely.

Sarah got another place immediately (so great is the demand) and in two days an indignant gentleman came ringing like mad at our door-bell. Honest Hoggins had stolen his silver, taken his baby-clothes, and now he came to us to know how it was we had ventured to vouch for such a creature!

She had simply told him that she had lived with us three months, and that we would give her a character, and he and his household were too lazy or too careless to verify her statement.

And now the clouds pass by, as black Sarah moves off the scene, and we arrive at the moral of this story; without which the foregoing would have no point; and this is, the entrance into our home of Norah, our young, gentle, amiable, beautiful girl, our cook and our friend.

Norah had tried marrying, and found that Love wouldn't boil the pot; that sewing-machine operators were not in great demand, and not well paid; that a sick husband was a bad thing to have in a penniless house; so she procured quarters for him, and prepared to pay his board by going out to service. She is happy with us, I am sure, and now that a widow's cap brings out in its snowy whiteness the dark gloss of her brown hair the chances of our separating are remote. We are a little selfish as regards Norah perhaps. We cannot but hope she will not marry again. It really does not seem to us that her lot in life should be that thankless one which she owns who plays the part of the strong vine that upholds the rotten oak.

"But granting that your Norah is a superior young woman, what is she, after all," you ask, "but a servant?"

And what are we all but servants? You, reader, are the servant to somebody. And I who write to you am your servant. You have a habit of buying books at certain seasons of the year, and to reach one of these seasons I must needs write early and late, and so serve you. I serve you gladly, it is true. I love to write. Ten books the size of this would not hold all I have to say to you at this very moment.

Again, I am advertised to lecture. I am tired; my head aches; I'd rather not. But I am a servant—contract signed and sealed, my liberty for a certain hour bought from me, my wages ready to be paid me when I shall earn them. Who shall doubt that I am a servant?

If I cannot serve you as well when I am married as when I was single, you will very naturally discharge me in spite of the strong signs of appreciation which you have hitherto shown me; and you will be quite right.

Thus it often happens that a woman must choose between marriage and service. Somewhere in the future let us hope there will be a state of affairs so millennial that these two things may not conflict with each other so sadly as they do in our day.

XVIII.

DID you ever have a day of complete discouragement? Of course, yes. Everybody has them. Longfellow says:

> "Into some hearts the rain must fall,
> Some days must be dark and dreary."

The rain has fallen in torrents for me to-day, though the sun has been shining gloriously in the heavens. I feel as if I had accomplished nothing. Yet I have written eighteen pages.

Eighteen pages about Love—and I feel as if I had been trying to dip up the ocean with a spoon. I crumple the eighteen pages in my hand and toss them in the fire which burns upon our hearth this cool evening in early spring.

How can people analyze you, Love? It seems to me that the more I write the farther I am away from any expression of you!

Love is so deep, so moving, so profound, that my mind stands with a helpless feeling, half awe, half despair, looking into the abysmal depths, in which my heart wanders as freely as a child in a ower-garden.

I cannot think that it is always she who loves most deeply who writes most clearly on this subject.

You know George Sand has analyzed the passion in its every stage; has pictured love spiritual, physical, moral, immoral, material and immaterial; yet her life has been such a record of free-love impurities that I cannot believe she ever had one glimpse of true love whispered to her by the voice of her own heart.

She has been beloved; no doubt of that. Jules Sandeau (for whom she left her husband, and a part of whose name she appropriated in literature) loved her dearly; Chopin madly; Alfred de Musset passionately.

She awakened so many sentiments in a man's breast; admiration for her beauty, her brilliant conversation, pride in her genius, honor for her magnificent literary work. All these drew men towards her. This man loved her because of all her attractions; that other for some one of them alone; and each and every one of these lovers she has laid on a dissecting-table, and opened every artery with her keen knife and laid bare its workings before her class of amazed students—her readers.

She has given us some rare pictures of love. If she had ever truly loved, could she have laid it on her page so clearly?

It was the current report in the literary circle in which I mingled in Paris (of which Thackeray was the shining light) that she drew men on to fall in love with her, one after another,—like those lovely nymphs in Rhine legend whom mortals love only to be destroyed,—that she might have a new experience to present to the public of this marvellous mystery of the human heart.

We are sitting around the Table, in the evening. I appeal to the circle.

"Come," I say. "My day's work has gone for nothing. You must help me out. Tell me something about Love. I will act as reporter of the meeting. Rebecca shall begin. Rebecca, what can you tell me about Love?"

Rebecca smiles in that quaint way of hers. "If you will tell me what Truth is," she says, "I will tell you what Love is."

"Worthy of a philosopher, Rebecca. Algie, it is your turn. Give me your idea of Love."

For his answer, Algie puts his arms about

my neck and gives me a rousing kiss on the cheek.

"Good boy! Now, husband!"

"Apropos of George Sand," says W., "I was looking at her portrait to-day, in the Brussels album. On the opposite page, is the portrait of Jules Sandeau, her romantic lover. They are recent portraits—I bought them in Paris last summer. They show me an old woman and an old man; and they are pathetic pictures to me—the pictures of two lonely, loveless old persons, to whom life must be a sad and fruitless thing. This, it seems to me, is a consideration with regard to Love, which all loose-minded persons overlook. It is overlooked by such persons as Mr. Trotman and Mrs. Freelove, in their disposition to make a virtue of that fickle and unstable disposition some people possess—to whom marriage is a galling bond because it holds them to a steadfast loyalty against which they naturally rebel. It needs no prophet to predict the old age of Mrs. Freelove. It will be loveless; and a loveless old age is dreadful to think upon. We can do without love in our younger days, when we are strong and self-reliant, and when the promise of love rests ever in the future. Even in middle age there is always room for hope, on the part of the person who is without love. But when one has reached old age, and is still a wanderer up and down the earth, companionless, childless, homeless, that must be bitter—and especially bitter if, besides, the poor old creature has to look back upon a life crowded with light loves."

I have known more than one such woman as this, and I always shudder when I see another treading the path where so many have been lost. Vanity is the root of this terrible error. A woman passes thirty, and is still a charming woman; men flock about her, and, to outrival early youth and beauty which surround her in the shape of young girls, she throws to her admirers an appetizing bait—an admission of her *almost* conversion to free-love principles. A fatal lure; fatal to the chances of young and innocent girls whose youth and innocence are as the healthful bread of life—men cast them aside and call for the hot brandy of vice—fatal thus to the men, but most fatal of all to the wretched tempter-woman who is sure to be loathed and flung away at last.

I have known of many so-called loves which braved society by an illegal alliance, and sought to command respect by promising to show the world a constancy which would amaze it. And a few years passed, and behold a bitter, soured couple, chafing under galling bonds, ashamed to look their children in the face, hating each other for having been the cause of this *faux pas*, longing to fly from their companion, but staying together because they were too proud to confess to the world that it was right after all, and they were wicked, sinful, and head-strong.

Sometimes an old coquette will have as many "*grandes passions*" on hand at once as a young girl has partners at her first ball. False to the core herself, she yet rails at men because of their inconstancy. I have heard such women talk in a way that turned me sick with disgust. I have known women of this sort who moved in the best society and kept up an outward show of respectability while they were carrying on correspondences with married men (they themselves also being married) and whom I have *seen* besot themselves with liquor and stench themselves with cigarettes, and then sit down in a half maudlin state and *curse* men for their infidelity; couple their abuse of the opposite sex with profanity, obscenity, and sacrilegious blasphemy, till I have wept tears of horror and pity for them.

Of course these women do not confess to absolute criminality; every "affair" is going to be the one affair of their lives *now;* and the next you hear is, if you happen to be so unfortunate as to be the receiver of their confidences, that *that* man was a heartless, faithless scoundrel, curse him! And there is another man on the carpet now invested with all the virtues—until his hour for disgust and loathing of the woman comes, and he too throws her off; and so goes on the weary round.

A woman may sin and marry and reform; purified by the holy love of a good man, upheld by his goodness and strength, she may lay her head on his shoulder and honestly look in his eyes and not quail before them, so long as she is true to him. This is a history often enacted in real life, often touchingly told in fiction. Wicked indeed would be the meddler who should dare to break up by calumny and slander such love and repentance as are here presented.

I honor the man whose love is strong enough to overlook the past of the woman to whom he has made up his mind to give his name, to whose hands he has resolved to trust his honor and rely upon her—spite of her past—to keep it untainted.

You have heard the story of the Marquis de Boissy; (I think that was his name, but if it was something else it doesn't matter) the French nobleman who married the Countess Guiccioli. The lady's name as given now was so piquantly celebrated that many titters and neck-stretchings were heard and seen when she made her appearance in society's gatherings.

"The Countess Guiccioli!" was more than once said in the hearing of Monsieur de Boissy, "Why is not that the lady who was the—ha! ha!—the particular *friend* of Lord Byron?"

"The same, sir," answered the Marquis, with a polite bow; then lifting his form to its most erect position and lightly tapping his sword-hilt, he added, "and I am the Marquis de Boissy, her husband."

I never heard that the wife proved false to this noble protection.

Poor railing woman! You who curse men

and their infidelity; who dare to sneer at the honesty and purity of all men; who lift your vile voice up and try to cast slurs on the great God, who could crush you, helpless worm, in the very instant of your blasphemies against Him, know now and forever that, spite of your concealment, this very language is the banner you fling out to the winds, which bears plainly stamped upon it the confession of your impurity, that all who run may read. Repent while there is time. Go and sin no more. Try to realize that *you* are the one who has been wicked; it may be that you have ruined the virtue of some pure man—there *are* such, spite of your weak, wicked and sickening ravings to the contrary—tens of thousands of them.

XIX.

"BUT you believe in divorce, I suppose?" sneered Mr. Trotman, with the air of a man who has put a staggerer of a question.

Yes, I believe in divorce, and I believe in removing a cancer with a knife.

The operation may kill you; but as life is

valueless when one has a cancer, one may as well risk getting cured by the surgeon's terrible knife--especially as, if the cancer continues, *it* will kill you.

When I look around and see the unhappiness which exists between certainly three-fourths of the married people I know, my only wonder is —not that so many people seek divorces, but that so few do.

"There!" says Mrs. Freelove, "my argument exactly. The whole system is wrong. Marriage is an absurd and cruel tyranny from which earth should be freed. Men and women should love when and whom they please. The most intimate relations ought to be taken on and put off at will."

It is a pet taunt with free-love women that no woman who has been obliged to submit to the cruel legal operation—divorce—has the right to object to their doctrines. As if divorce and free-love had of necessity anything in common! Divorce and free-love are no more allied than marriage and free-love; for one need not to be divorced in order to commit free-love—since that is the euphemism now employed. Such an imputation is enough to make the bones of every dead divorced woman turn in the grave—beginning with the chaste and lovely Josephine de Beauharnais, divorced wife of the first Napoleon.

There is an American woman, well known to many who will read this book, and honored by every good and true man and woman who does know her, who has been three times married, and twice divorced. She is a good and pure woman, now preaching the gospel—a noble woman, whom any household might be glad to welcome under its rooftree—a most unfortunate woman, whose sorrowful history might almost wring tears from a heart of stone. Mrs. Free-love and her clan profess to feel mighty fine indignation at the fact that *this* woman should repudiate them, scoff at their doctrines, pronounce their teachings wicked and pernicious. But the plain truth is that this woman—spite of her three marriages—is purer than any virgin who should only entertain free-love doctrines, believe them, intend to follow them.

You ask perhaps how it is that a good woman should have thrown herself into three marriages; this is not even pathetic, it is almost ludicrous.

I knew this woman when I was a child. She

was a great beauty, and a sweet poet. She was married at sixteen to a pork-packer, who, report said, treated her worse than one of his own hogs. Set free from him, she again married, after a time. She was young, beautiful and, she hungered for affection. A man who I am told was as beautiful and as gifted as herself won her love; but he was—I think there can be little doubt—Don Juan redivivus. Insulted, betrayed, polluted by his atmosphere of debauch, she again appealed to the law to loose this tie. She was heart-broken. Years passed; and then a blessed, gray-haired man, twenty years her senior, gave her his name, his protecting care, the blessing of his love. You should hear this story from her own lips to feel its full significance. I think the severest moralist among you would not hesitate to say, "Poor woman, I do not blame you."

I am not well enough acquainted with its details to feel warranted in attempting to tell her story, or to illustrate how it may have been with her, in the two painful, mistaken alliances she was led to make, before she married the good man who blessed her life, and whom she mourns henceforth in perpetual widowhood.

I have seen so much shame and so much misery arise out of those love-matches which are made in youth's heat, when, the judgment immature, the heart untried, life all untasted, two mad creatures rush into each other's arms, like two chemicals in a laboratory! When the explosion is over, the smoke subsides, and the heart's fury calms, then the two mad creatures look into each other's faces and see what fools they have been. "And to think that I am joined to this man for life!" exclaims the woman. "A pretty millstone I've tied around my neck!" says the husband. And thenceforth they are obliged to trudge along through life together, through joy and sorrow, weal and woe, in relations of closest intimacy till death shall part them.

Now in regard to a match of this sort, I hope I shall not be considered unchristianlike if I respectfully decline to believe it was made in heaven. I know of several just such, that were made in a boarding-house where I lived, and very unhappy they proved.

One—ah me, how well I remember it! was of a young girl, extremely guileless and unworldly, who, when less than seventeen years old, "fell in love" with a man who dropped in one day to board where she did. It was at a small and uncomfortable hotel on Broadway, which everybody in it hated, but endured because it was cheap. Of course he fell in love with her first—wooed her with that delightful abandon which prevails in boarding-houses and cheap hotels, and finally gained her heart—for the time, that is. He represented himself as a wealthy Southerner, at present rather cramped for money from some cause or other, but a wealthy man for all that, who would take care of her from that time forth, provide her with every comfort, and of course relieve her from all labor. The young girl was earning fifteen dollars a week. She gave up her situation, and married him.

Her family did not attempt to look into the young man's character and antecedents. In the first place they knew nobody who knew him; in the second place, such were his insinuating ways, that they bestowed their fullest confidence in him, and would not have believed anything against him if they had heard it. So this couple were made one flesh—at least a minister said so, and stated in a hurried voice (he had an invitation up town and was in a hurry), that no man should put asunder what God had joined together.

And if God had really joined them together, it would have been a heinous crime for any man to put them asunder; but, knowing the circumstances of the case thoroughly as I do, I refuse to believe that God had anything to do with such a hasty, ill-advised, ill-assorted, and altogether wretched marriage.

The wealthy Southerner was proved to be neither wealthy, nor a Southerner, nor a gentleman; but a miserable gambler, without an honest dollar in his pocket, nor an honest idea in his head, nor an honest sentiment in his heart. You may fancy the girl's horror on awakening to these facts, as well as to the knowledge that her husband's love for her was a species of hot-blooded fever which died out completely after three months of matrimony. But the saddest discovery of all was the discovery of her own feelings concerning the man to whom she was joined for life. The veil dropped from her eyes, and showed her the appalling truth—that she hated her husband.

Will anybody say this match was made in

heaven? Were these people really joined by God? I think it blasphemy to say so.

If it be that Satan has anything to do with making disjointed marriages—as he no doubt has with every kind of sin—I should say *he* was the prime-mover in joining these people.

Ten thousand such marriages take place every year. In their train they bring untold agonies, remorse, chafing under the galling yoke and not unfrequently insanity, infamy and violent death.

What then? Is the fault with *marriage?* Shall we then condemn *marriage?*

Why, you poor, trivial creature, you might as well infer that it is the fault of *religion* that a hypocrite derives no good from his religious professions. You might as well condemn *truth* because you, having heard that truth lay at the bottom of a well, had jumped into a well in search of it, and drowned yourself.

When marriage fails to be a blessing to us, the fault lies primarily in ourselves. We are the sufferers from our own folly, our own vanity, our own weakness or wickedness. The cancer has grown in our breasts, because we ourselves planted it there.

When Mrs. Freelove assails marriage, she

assails an institution as essential to our civilization as law itself. If you can safely abolish all law, then you can abolish marriage.

—Ah, but this is not all—no, no! When I contemplate the idea of your abolishing the marriage of people who love—and I know many such—even to repealing the *law* which makes it a virtue in both husband and wife to obey the promptings of their natures—I feel that you would rob them of something I and they cannot name, but for which there is no recompense! Why, rash iconoclast, people who love and are married kiss with joy the gyve which binds them together!

There is no resisting Love, when Heaven smiles upon the lovers. Not all the votes that were ever cast, from Washington's day down to Tweed's,—and counting the repeating done, this is a considerable number,—will ever change this fact. Free-love reformers might as well try to legislate child-bearing to the other sex as to hope to change a sentiment as immutable as death.

My only conception of God is—not the Great Jehovah who rules the spheres, and holds the waters in the hollow of his hand—but a good Father who will love me, and rest me.

A person who knew Wilberforce once told me that the only way he could picture to himself Christ was to say to himself, "Jesus is Wilberforce millions of times improved. And He will love me and comfort me as Wilberforce did—but immeasurably more."

In fact, there is nothing on earth worth living for but love; nothing so beautiful, nothing so rare. Give it as freely as you can—give it to mother, father, sister, brother, child, friend—but you can give it but once to a husband.

XX.

In some way, somehow, somewhere, a woman must be her husband's partner—or take the consequence: contempt. To what degree, and in what kind, depends on many circumstances.

For example, a man may be so splendidly framed by his Maker, that he is capable of being *just*. There are such men in the world; but they are rare. Such a man may perceive that his wife, while lacking in certain qualities wherein he is strong, equalizes her lack therein by the possession of other qualities wherein he is weak. This, to begin with, opens the window which ventilates a home with pure air, in which contempt cannot live.

Happy is the lot of the wife whose marriage bond was wrought in heaven! For the condition of all such, God be praised! They have no need of the benefits which attach to ability to care for one's self, until—ah, yes! until the good husband dies, or changes from goodness into its reverse—as it is in the nature of poor humanity to do—until the yoke presses hard on the feeble neck, and the woman realizes that bitter is the lot of woman. When she lays her husband in the grave—either in the actual graveyard mould of physical death, or the tomb of dead virtue, dead faithfulness, dead honor, the weeds of drunkenness, debauchery, and shame rioting over him—then, when the question arises "How to earn my own and my children's daily bread," she learns the misfortune of being a dependent woman.

If the fault were simply in woman as woman, instead of in the *position* of woman, there would be less to say. But, I indignantly deny that woman's weakness is in her sex. The refutation of this libel is found in ten thousand instances, where woman has risen above her common position of dependence, and has proved herself equal to such work as man is equal to.

Blessed be the woman who is wedded to manhood, honor, intelligence, virtue, justice! But, shame upon the woman who is thus blest, if she, in a selfishness which is beyond all other selfishness on earth, shall be false to the spirit of grand and beneficent principle! So one might cry, "*I* have no need of charity—away with charity! charity is insolence to me!" But others may need it.

Many women, from sheer mental laziness, are opposed to any improvement in the condition of their sex. They look over the newspapers, and, being unable to comprehend clearly the drift of certain great questions, because they have never taken the pains to study them, they think political and social science an occult mystery, which it would be hopeless in them to ever dream of penetrating. So they determine not to expose their own ignorance, but to conceal it under a mean cry of—"Woman's sphere is the kitchen! Any woman is unsexed who meddles with higher questions than soup and stuffing."

Sometimes they affect a sweet simplicity, and simper something like this:

"Oh, those coarse creatures who have brains in their heads! I've not got any brains in my head, so I'm not coarse. I'm a sweet and simple little idiot that don't know whether politics is something to drink or a sort of garment. I hear so much about turn-coats, you know. He! he! I don't know anything. Don't you admire me, sir?"

And this woman finds men who pat her on the head, as they would any other frisky little puppy, male or female, quadruped or biped.

No doubt the Turkish seraglio slave-woman thinks her degraded position the proper sphere for her sex, and would hoot at any one who proposed a change in that position. No doubt she would declare a woman "unsexed" who should dare to violate the old established routine of life there, and pronounce the bowstring the proper reward for her immodest conduct in seeking a larger liberty.

And apropos of this, an anecdote:

When I was residing in Paris, a dressmaker, who used to work for me, received one day a large order for dresses for some oriental women kept in a seraglio in Algiers. The dress—of which patterns were sent her—consisted of a loose gored sack, open in front, falling to the knee, and flowing trousers underneath this, gathered at the ankle. Everything was to be made of the most expensive material—silk, satin, gauze, gossamer—and it was stipulated that the lining of both trousers and sack was to be as rich, costly, and perfectly finished off as the outside.

The job was a profitable one, and to be sure of pleasing her employers and thus securing further custom from them, the dressmaker sent her eldest daughter (a young married woman) to Algiers, to deliver the articles. When she returned, Marie told me that the Algerian women received their things like babies—clapping their hands and dancing with joy over them. But they presently turned their attention to the woman who brought them; and when they found she had walked through the streets without a veil, such as they wore around their heads, leaving nothing but their eyes visible, they called her all sorts of vile names, charged her with being lost to virtue, slapped her face, and turned her out of their presence.

It is but a narrow intelligence which is unable

to separate the aims of honor-loving and virtue-cherishing women from those of free-love advocates, merely because they both believe in changes in woman's status. God knows, I wage no war upon the comfortable lot she occupies, whose husband's love is all to her, and enough for all her wants. Rest contented in your pleasant nest, dear! But don't shake your pretty little head disapprovingly at women whose objects in life are beneficent for your sex, however little you may think they are for you. Your time of need may come, it is true. I hope it may not. But if it should, I hope also that you may not find yourself unable to earn your livelihood.

There are undoubtedly men in the world who do not want their wives to work. And if, in the great scheme of existence, there were one such man to marry every woman, there would be less occasion for the discussion of woman's needs. Yet if there be one woman in this world, who hath no such husband to save her from the necessity of toil, that one woman's case is to be provided for in some other way.

And what is the fact?

Why the fact is that there are thousands and

thousands of such women. The avenues of labor are thronged with such women, struggling with inefficient powers against the hard fate of poverty, which is always crowding them into temptation's paths; and the grand army of sin and shame is constantly recruited from their ranks

---

XXI.

AND motherhood! What of this question of child-bearing, and child-tending, which comes with marriage?

If we were living in a state of ideal civilization, I should not have to put on record the hard truths which belong to this subject. I should be able to speak of motherhood sweetly, poetically, as the holy and blessed thing it is, and draw you such fair pictures of the ideal mother and child as should make your heart glad with admiration. But the truth is, motherhood is in this day and country practically received as a doubtful blessing by most women. Why?

"It isn't the first of it I care so much about," said an expectant mother to me recently, "but it is the long years—three, four, or five—during which I must be at the mercy of the child."

It is because there is so much slavery put on the mother which need not be put there, that so many women look forward with something very like dread to the prospect of motherhood.

I have before printed my views on the absurdity of insisting that a strong, active-brained, labor-competent woman, should be compelled by the force of custom to sit for hours holding a baby on her knees to the exclusion of every other employment.

I have been thought hard in this matter—lacking in that innate adoration of babyhood which should inspire the soul of every true woman.

But those who think I can see no charms in babyhood, know not my inmost heart. I suppose I am as instinctively an idolater in this sphere as most women are.

But because I love Baby, I would serve him. I see that Baby is not so flourishing an institution in these days, and in this country, as he was in other days, and is in some other countries. And the reason may be perceived by the naked eye, by any intelligent person who will look at it without green goggles of prejudice on. In those other countries Baby is not the incubus upon woman's energies that he is in this country.

A money-earning European mother would never think of giving up her employment to sit and hold her baby. I know that there have been many abuses relating to paid baby-tending in Europe; but if we should adopt anything like their system, we could enact such laws as European mistakes have taught us to be necessary. But these abuses can only exist when the mother is so unfortunate as to be obliged to put her child out in the country—away from her—to nurse, along with a number of other babies who are all expected to eke out a scanty sustenance from the bosom of a common nurse-mother. I am speaking now on behalf of dress-makers, milliners, copyists, and a large number of women engaged in employment which they do at home, but which custom exacts they shall immediately relinquish when baby comes—leaving the getting of very necessary income to devote their whole time to holding baby on their knees, or getting down on the floor and playing with him.

There are so many poor women and girls in this world—so many classes to whom a dollar is a large sum—that I hold it to be the duty of every woman who can do service in a high path of labor, to hire some poorer woman to perform the necessary details of a lower one. A woman who is capable of earning five dollars by her work for half an hour, is a dunce if she devotes that half-hour to saving fifty cents. It is all wrong, this sort of economy. I myself have kept the printer waiting while I was preparing clothes for the wash; I have spent two whole days turning and twisting an old dress, when I might have made enough to buy me a new one and pay for the making of it by writing a newspaper article. These were the mistakes which opened my eyes and made me see the folly which I would be glad to keep other women from running into. My preparing of the clothes for the wash was not one whit better, and my re-making of the old dress was not so good, as would have been that of some woman who was incapable of writing the magazine article, and to whom but a portion of the money I earned by the other and more congenial work would have been a God-send.

Let the husband of the woman who is expecting to be a mother say to her, "Now dear, come what may, you shall have a nurse-girl to help you take care of that baby. Under your eye a girl a dozen years old, whose services may be had for a trifle, will help amazingly to relieve you of the ceaseless fatigue and care."

Such a girl can, at the beginning, rock a cradle and run certain errands which a baby always brings; and as baby grows older the nurse-girl can amuse him during the long hours; she can play on the floor with him, set up and knock down continuous bricks for him, and play with him just as skilfully as you can.

When baby is sick or hungry, then mother is wanted, and nobody can take her place; but when the little stomach is full to repletion, when no pin obtrudes itself and aches are forgotten, then mother may well busy her adult hands and brain with needful, thoughtful work, and leave a nurse to care for baby—especially if she herself is in the same room.

In looking at Europe through the goggles of

prejudice, American women have seen a great many ugly things which are not visible to the naked eye.

They have seen that European mothers are heartless, frivolous, wicked—that they have no serious conception of the importance of motherhood, the duties of child-rearing, the blessed privilege of devoting one's self entirely to Baby.

Now let us fly—only for a paragraph or two—to France. Turning back a few pages of life's book you may see her who now writes these lines to you, standing at the bedside of a young French wife. This lady, during three-quarters of a year has held herself as a special agent of God, the object of His more than common care, the medium through which His greatest marvel is to be performed. Also, she has held that medium sacred. She has lived with special regard to the life which is to be. Her food has been chosen judiciously; her exercise has been out in the air. She has bathed tri-weekly in luke-warm water, lying in the healthfully relaxing bath a half an hour each time. She has avoided all excitements, all anger, all ill-temper, all feverish balls or parties. But tranquil amusement has been constant; she must be diverted. "It is important, because the child's mind is forming at the same time as its body," says her husband. "We desire our child to have a cheerful temperament."

* * * * * * * *

"It is finished! It is happily terminated!" cries out the cheery, valuable midwife. "It's not more difficult than that. *Allons! courage*, little mama! *Bon jour*, mademoiselle! How dost thou find thyself? There's thy little mama lying on that bed. How dost thou find her—to thy liking? Come, little mother, it is an admirable little daughter that the good God has sent us. God be praised!"

Four days afterward the little mother tells me she feels as if she'd like to scrub the floor. Happily, she is not allowed. Old traditions prevail even with the most sensible people. Nine days must pass before she leaves her room; but she is sitting up and moving about before that.

And the little daughter?—the beloved angel of the good God?

Ah, she if you please is already forming her opinion of her future place of residence. She is promenading up and down the Champs Elysées, or around the church of the Madeleine, or sauntering the length of the Boulevards, when she is three days old.

On a pillow. In the arms of a nurse. To be sure. But think of it! Three days old, and cold weather!

And every day, rain or shine, cold or warm, this admirable little daughter disports herself in the air almost the whole day long. From her birth she is outdoors. As she grows older she runs, she jumps, she romps, she enjoys life to the full. And spite of this early training I never heard that the manners of a Frenchwoman were lacking in elegance or even femininity.

"These are rich people's children. How do the poor do?"

They manage otherwise—but they manage. That any child—of parents no matter how poor—should remain cooped up within doors for even one whole day would seem to the French mind, something very like a catastrophe.

And you know how it is with the English. If you do not, wait until you go to the beautiful isle by the sea. There shall you see in the public parks little girls and boys mounted on

Shetland ponies about the size of Newfoundland dogs, galloping from one end of Rotten Row to the other, pictures of health, beauty and innocence. There shall you see young ladies rowing, swimming, following the hounds mounted on mettlesome chargers, leaping five-barred gates and taking ten-mile walks as a daily constitutional. And the red cheeks, and the hard, healthy flesh! How I long for these for my countrywomen, North and South, East and West! Can we not have them? What's to prevent?

"The red cheeks are an affair of climate."

It may be so; but the healthy body is not. That is an affair of regular habits, of pure air, of vigorous out-door exercise. We can have all these.

Let us have them. Women in the rural districts, get, each of you, a pair of strong boots and make it a duty like any other to walk at least two or three miles every day! Women of the city, who can walk in any weather over miles and miles of well-paved streets, let not the fear of being seen in an old dress keep you within, any day in the year. It is so easy to explain it to any one of whose opinion you stand in awe. "I came out, bad as the weather is, for my constitutional." And not one but will say "Sensible woman, to care for her health."

And let these be laws which you yourself, good mother, make for your girl children from their earliest youth. Open their little minds to the sweet knowledge that feet were made to scamper with, arms were made to swing by, mouths were made to breathe fresh air through, nostrils to snuff it up with, ears are organs with which to listen to song-birds, eyes are organs with which to gaze upon the glory of God's blue heaven, unobstructed by a window-pane.

XXII.

DID you ever know an expectant mother who wanted a girl? No, I'll answer for it. Husband "wants a boy" and so does she.

Nevertheless, in this matter as in all others, God disposes; and the nurse cries from behind her cap-frill "Oh, sir, you've got such a *dear* little daughter!"

A daughter! Why, he and wife had counted on

a son; had even settled what they should name him; nay, they had gone further—they had called him William after his rich uncle, who was so delighted that he forthwith died and left the child all his money. But a daughter!—oh! the golden dream vanishes as abruptly as did that of the farmer's daughter who had reckoned up even to a husband out of the basket of eggs she was carrying on her head, and broke them all as she curtseying tossed her silly noddle to decline a mythical rival.

A daughter! why they made sure it would be a son! This aversion to a feminine baby would indicate that we resemble the Chinese more closely than we think.

However, missie is born. What are you going to do about it? You can't send her back where she came from. One reason is that you don't know where she came from. At any rate, she is here. Trim her with laces, swathe her in fine linen. She is only a little more helpless now than she will be as a woman.

In the cradle there is no distinction of sex. Tiny man will amuse himself with a string of empty spools or an india-rubber doll as well as missie; and spite of her pride in his sex mamma will scarcely give her three-months-old boy gun, pistol, or drum as he lies squirming in his crib. For a period at least the sexes are equal; there is no disadvantage in being a girl.

But speed me a year; and I will show you already unmistakable signs of the manship of master. His hair is parted to one side. He's a boy. He's papa's MAN; he's mamma's BOY! he's lord of all he surveys.

So anxious are his parents that the world shall know that this bit of humanity is not that inferior thing, a girl, but that he has undoubted right to belong to the powerful tribe of mascu-lines, that, before he can do much more than stagger (the full perfection of this he acquires later in life), you shall hear the mother telling of her plans for putting him in trousers. "He's such a boy," "he's a *regular* boy, you know;" and a regular boy he remains to the proud mother's heart until the time comes when that heart is torn with the knowledge that he is an irregular one.

In England an arbitrary decree of baby caps says to the world, "He is the man!" for a rosetted cap means boy baby, and a rosetteless cap turns up its contemptuous frills at the girl.

Do I accuse mothers of lack of love for their girl-children? God forbid. And forbid it also the gentle remembrance of my own dear mother who tenderly reared and loved *six* daughters!

But my accusation is against the foolish distinctions made, in a thousand seemingly unimportant ways, between these two creatures whom God made with equal care, equal love; to whom together he gave the world; to whom together he has promised life everlasting.

"Why what can I do?" says a young mother. "I don't make the difference between my children. My boy is a real *boy*. He says *he wouldn't be a girl for anything.*"

Who taught him to say such an absurd and insolent thing? who encouraged him thus to insult his mother?

Generally his mother—but particularly his father.

It is such good fun to cast slurs on the sex. Is a boy of a quiet and retiring turn of mind? Oh, shame him out of that—that's so like a *girl!* Is he timid? Then be sure you avoid condemning timidity for itself, but only because it is a distinguishing quality of a *girl*. Is he a cry-baby? Then never trouble yourself to explain that all cry-babies are nuisances, but say to him, with disdainful lip and curling nostril, "Eh, a cry-baby! Ain't you ashamed! Just like a *girl!*" And father, mother and child give in chorus one long sneer of contempt.

Nor does it in the least matter that your little girl sitting there shall hear all this.

Thus she early learns that mean and contemptible qualities are her birthwrong. Nor is she ever encouraged to cast them aside as unworthy. She is a girl. They belong to her sex.

I have known boy babies of whose acquaintance I was ashamed. They were so dastardly that I have cut them in public. They were mean, sneaking, snivelling, weak creatures; yet by dint of earnest urging by loving mothers, whose constant aim it was to hold up to them the high qualities which manhood required of them, these boy creatures succeeded at last in throwing aside many of the contemptible weaknesses which were evidently born in them and ripened into strong, self-reliant, and worthy men.

If I were permitted to make the laws of the nursery, I would begin with this:

Section I. In no boy-baby exchange shall the stock of girl-babyhood be quoted below par.

Section II. Children shall only be guided toward what is good, pure and true, not toward what is becoming to their sex. Cowardice, weakness, lack of fortitude and all that is wicked or weak is to be shunned because it is wicked and weak, and not because it is girlish or boyish.

XXIII.

I WONDER what makes baby cry so? A pin?

But you cry pin, pin, and there is no pin. All strings, sensible mother, or buttons, or, better still, a few stitches done freshly every morning.

"Then *what* makes baby cry? Ah, to be sure—hungry!"

And nature's fount—or the apothecary's, the bottle—is thrust in baby's mouth until she fairly spits it out.

Did it ever strike you that your baby is bored

with your society? that she has had enough of you, as you sometimes think you have had of her?

Then it is time to vary the monotony by introducing new elements. Invite one of your neighbor's babies in, and give the children their first sociable by laying them down on the bed or the floor together. My word for it, presently you will hear them crow and chirp, and you will see them clap their chubby hands together, and even make an effort to grasp each other's. The observations of hundreds of watchful eyes will testify to the truth of this statement: that the very youngest children often long for the society of those of their own age, and nothing less than that will make them happy.

Every nurse knows that it is far easier to take care of two or even three children than one. The reason is that a child alone is a tyrant; his helplessness is his power; he rules all around him with a rod of iron. I have seen a woman with accomplishments enough to charm a court circle, at her wit's end to provide amusement for her own baby.

But put another child along with this child; then baby learns its first lesson of duty to society. He (or she) stands more in awe of that other baby than he (or she) does of an entire grown household.

"Stop making that noise, Willie," said Clarisse to her boy aged three years; "we are talking."

"Oo stop talking," was the answer. "I must make this noise."

He is ringing the dinner-bell at nine o'clock in the morning.

And by what method of reasoning are you to convince that boy that our talking (about bonnets, I confess) is any more important than his bell-ringing? Or that we have any right to a monopoly of noises in the house, which so far as he knows belongs entirely to him? Clarisse should early have explained this important point to him. It would have been simple at the very beginning. The trouble is that a young child is humored so outrageously that he soon learns to look upon his rights as paramount to all others. No matter what fine new toy or book is presented to any other child in the house, if Baby cries for it he must have it. "*Do* give it to him, you selfish girl! Do give it to your little baby brother."

Oh, the throngs of little martyrs all over the world to tyrant baby!

I mind me of a household where a boy baby deigned to make his appearance. He was the first-born; a little beauty, really, in other eyes than those of his parents, and time has improved his character until he is now as good as he is good-looking. But you never would have thought such a change could possibly come about; for from the time he was one month old until he passed his sixth year, I think he was as bad a child as ever lived.

"I must be amoosed," he would roar. "Amoose me!" and he would jerk your book out of your hand, and kick it about the floor.

"My dear, why *don't* you amuse that child?" would cry the husband. "How any one can sit quietly by reading when that child wants to be amused is more than I can understand! Do something to amuse him!"

"But, Fred, I am sewing on my new dress now, which you want me to have done in time to wear to church on Sunday."

"Put it away. Stay at home from church."

"I want to be amoosed!" screamed the boy by this time, indulging in a flood of tears "just like a girl."

"Yes, darling; yes, *swe-e-t!*" cried wife, husband and friend in chorus.

But how to accomplish this difficult task? Master was fastidious. No, he didn't want to ride a jack-horse to Banbury Cross; no, he wouldn't have the bear come and eat him (said bear being his mother down on all fours, creeping up to him wagging her head and roaring idiotically—and when she got close, having him thrust his naughty little fist in her face for recompense); no, he didn't want his whip, nor any of the expensive and ingenious toys which had been bought, at any sacrifice, for him; no —ah yes—he *would* make a railroad train!

A railroad train consisted of every chair in the house being fastened together with twine; and included the services of at least one adult to sit motionless for hours and cry out "tchew! tchew!"—this passing muster as the voice of the steam-engine.

But if visitors came and even one of those chairs was wanted, what a yelling, shrieking, altogether hideous scene that boy would make! It was not only annoying, it was disgraceful.

One day when the washerwoman came with her basketful of clean linen, a tablecloth was found to be torn; and the woman said "I didn't do it, the little boy must have done it."

He couldn't have been more offended if she had called him a girl. He raged. And his sensible parents laughed in admiration of this sweet exhibition of his temper; and consoled him for the indignity which had been (justly enough, no doubt) put upon him by saying, in that mellifluous and elevated language which inane parents deem necessary to use when speaking to their children:

"Did ze nasty wasserwoman say little boy tory tablecloss? Oh, ze nassy, baddy wasserwoman! Little boy give it to her next time she tums. Little boy knock her over ze head, wissy broomstick."

He needed no second telling. For a week he kept that idea in his mind. When the laundress appeared he walked out deliberately after the broomstick, and coming quietly in, went up behind her and rapped her over the pate such a blow that it was a mercy he didn't break it.

Fancy the tableau! An inoffensive washer-woman — a good washerwoman, of virtuous morals and high clear-starching abilities—to be broomsticked on sight by your first-born, whom you have encouraged to the deed!

There were worse consequences than the two weeks' soiled clothes lying around the house, seeking whom they might be washed by. The story seemed so humorous to the good parents —who "never thought he *would* do such a thing! wasn't it *too* cunning?"—that by-and-by the boy began to think that he had developed a special talent in that line, and claiming the broomstick as his property, rapped every one in the house with it, until he felt encouraged to try it on his father, who, never expecting this, with masculine consistency, thrashed him.

What happened to this little rogue to redeem him?

A sister.

Yes, that sister happened and redeemed him. I do not mean romantically, you understand.

At five or six years old a boy's romantic nature is not largely developed. But the sister belonged to the child-world, like himself, and she showed him that though grown people had no rights he was bound to respect, yet she and other children had.

XXIV.

I SAID the other day to a friend who has a darling and be-petted boy of three years old, "How fortunate it is that that child does not pass at one step from this period of being humored in every fancy, of being encouraged in every whim, to that desperate battle of life awaiting him when he must fight for his bread, for his good name, for his position, for his religion."

"Yes," she said. "And it is difficult for me to realize that he will ever be a man. You know to us he seems so truly like an angel that I sometimes tremble for fear God will suddenly claim him; but if he lives, year by year he will lose his babyish sweetness, grow less interesting, have a will of his own, be naughty perhaps and we shall be obliged to punish him; then he will go to school, become absorbed in his studies, little by little detaching himself from us—and then! there he is a man and we are no longer those powerful lawgivers 'father' and 'mother;' we are simply the 'old folks.'"

Lawgivers! Ay, that's the word! The general run of parents seem to know only two states of existence: the first, when they are simply baby worshippers; the second, when they expect their children to become abject slaves of them, the parents.

How easy it is to tell what state of feeling exists in a household between parents and children, only by observing how the latter act when the former are present! Could anything be more depressing than to be an inmate of a home where the children are afraid to speak above a whisper when "father is in the room"—where "father's coming!" is the signal for as general a scattering, a rushing "to arms" of good behavior as the terrible cry "the enemy!" is to an army which fancied itself secure.

In such a household as this I scarcely know which to pity most—the parents who lose the delicious enjoyment of intercourse with young minds so much fresher and purer than their own—or the children whose recollection of their parents, instead of being in after years a source of blissful delight, is to be clouded by a dark vision of two grown-up tyrants, whose comfort and quietude were purchased at the cost of every innocent amusement of children.

None of our circle is happier in sitting about the Table than our boy Algie. He feels that his individuality is just as much respected there as it would be if he were fifty years old instead of fifteen. We try to avoid all show of authority with him as much as possible. We try to cultivate in him a spirit of manly self-respect, which will make him fear to do an unmanly thing, for his own sake. We would no more snub him than we would snub Rebecca.

You may see evidences in this small man of a rare sense of honor, and of appreciation of his place in our life—not as a serf, nor as a creature to be curbed, nor one to be put under restraint because of his youth—but as a companion and friend, a person to whom we look for comfort, cheer, and good-fellowship.

Perhaps an incident will illustrate Algie's character in this regard:

One day last winter he remembered that he had his father's promise that he might go skating. It was Saturday and he was home from school. I suppose the little gentleman had thought about it all the week; he is a beautiful skater and the Rink on Saturdays is crowded with children, and Algie's fancy skating is always admired. Why, once when he was cutting initials and making roses and doing all sorts of "big things on ice," a lot of elegant people, girls, boys, and grown folks, clustered around and looked at him, and when he finished they all clapped their hands and cried *bravo!* in a way that would have pleased an opera singer. So you may easily understand that he looked forward eagerly to Saturday and skating. He had been watching the weather all the time, and hoping it wouldn't thaw.

But lo and behold! when Saturday came and he put on his overcoat and took his skates in one hand and his cap in the other and went up to his father and said:

"Well, papa, I suppose I may go skating now, mayn't I? You promised me I might, you know."

Oh dear, here was a bad job! His papa was overwhelmed with work, wanted him very much indeed. He was up to his eyes in a sort of work which Algie was very handy at, and had been counting on this Saturday when he should have his boy's help. A shade of disappointment crept over his face, which Algie noted anxiously.

But our man is as honorable as our boy.

"If I promised you, Algie, that's the end of it. I wanted you so very much this afternoon! All right. You can go."

Algie went.

Where? why, to the cupboard and hung up his overcoat and cap, and put away his skates, and then came back with his sweet face bright as sunshine, and laying his arm around his father's shoulder affectionately, he said:

"What was it you wanted me to do, papa?"

It cost the boy a mighty effort to do this, and it was a nobler act than it may seem, here on my page. For Algie knew perfectly well that he was under no sort of compulsion—it was his right to go skating, and he knew that his rights were sacred in that house. But, much as he loved his favorite pastime, he loved the happiness of that home more, and he could not do anything to mar it.

Algie, if he were allowed, would ask nothing better than to be permitted constantly to furnish amusement for the whole household. He contributes his share to the attractions of our home, and enters into the question of the hanging of a new picture, or the training of a freshly-acquired flower, or the arrangement of a newly-furnished chamber, with as much gusto as any of us. The other day he brought us in such a pretty thing—a bottle, all covered and running over with a thick growth of beautiful living green. Oh, so pretty!' What an ornament it is to our Table!

He found out the secret of making this from another boy; and then he took the first thing that came to hand—a cracked bottle which he saw was of a graceful shape, with fat body and slender neck; and he got his Aunt Rebecca to sew two or three layers of flannel all over it and tightly fitting its form. Then he took a few cents' worth of curling cress seed and soaked it over night; next morning he spread the sticky seed all over the wet bottle—planted it, you might say, in the flannel. Then he stood the bottle in a saucer full of water and placed it in the sunshine; and every day as frequently as he found time he basted the bottle with water in a spoon—just as Norah does the roast, with the gravy. And the seed sprouted and covered the whole bottle with its bright luxuriance, and gave us for our dear Table, from our dear boy, a thing of beauty and a joy for several weeks—during which time everybody in the house is trying the experiment, and we shall soon have more than we know what to do with.

XXV.

I SHOULD very much like to see forever abolished the absurd notion that athletic sports should be confined to boys. If a girl feels a desire to climb fences, let her climb; if she wants to play marbles or toss jackstones, let her do these "unfeminine" things. But why unfeminine? Have marbles or jackstones any sex?

On the other hand, if a boy feels like learning to crochet or do worsted-work, let not these tastes be interfered with.

You smile at the idea of any healthy, hearty, wide-awake boy wanting to work in worsted! But you don't smile at the idea of a healthy, wide-awake girl doing it. On the contrary, "that's her sphere."

Chinese ruts, I tell you! It is no more absurd for a boy to embroider on Penelope canvas than it is for a man to measure calico and ribbons.

Two of the choicest gifts I had last Christmas were bookmarks of Bristol-board elaborately embroidered in split zephyr. Both were done by splendid boy friends of mine, one seven years old, the other thirteen. Their mothers are sensible women, not governed by arbitrary notions of the sexuality of employments.

And the boys don't care a farthing about great social questions, but say that it's real fun of a rainy day to sit down and work book-marks.

At the same time, if a boy would rather dig in the dirt than amuse himself with bright-hued wool, I would let him, with all my heart. And I would let a girl have the same privilege.

The cry which greets the girl as soon as she is able to comprehend anything more difficult of comprehension than pap and a perambulator is this: Be a Lady!

Liberally translated this means, Be a colorless, lifeless, aimless dough doll; be a spiritless, cowardly feminine machine; an ignoble, narrow-minded breathing apparatus.

What is it to be a lady? Or rather what should it be?

It should be to be stronger, nobler, more self-reliant than the common run; better educated, bigger hearted, larger brained; with mind to conceive, hands to execute.

And how can any girl obtain that first desideratum for ladyhood, health, if outdoor exercises are denied her?

"Oh, I don't want my girl to be a romp," says Mamma; "she gets exercise enough. She is taking Calisthenic lessons."

A government is best governed which is least governed. Exercise is healthiest which is not taught.

I joined a Calisthenic class once. It was for ladies and children; the two helpless classes—*les Imbéciles!*

The Bloomer costume was recommended to us, but it was not indispensable. Consequently it was a motley group which assembled twice a week in a large bare hall, where an out-of-tune piano showed its attenuated legs—so thin as to suggest that it needed Calisthenic exercise or something else to put vigor in them. The piano jingled—ti tum ti tum—under the emaciated fingers of a pale and worn woman; and *les Imbéciles* went and took their places like four-and-twenty blackbirds all in a row.

Provided with wooden dumb-bells about as heavy as gourds, these poor seekers for health and strength lifted their weak arms up and down—up and down—in time to the music. They stepped backward, they stepped forward; to the right, to the left; keeping their anxious eyes on the lady who stood in front of them to see that they did as she did.

"March!" cries the teacher; and they pro ceed to march. They tread on each other's heels; they turn the wrong way; they close up and squeeze the smaller children till the smaller children squeal and struggle to save themselves from being smothered; some few drop their dumb-bells on their neighbors' indignant toes; about half the marchers give up and retreat to benches; and oftener than not the whole class breaks up in disorder.

An awkward squad, you say? Yes, and an unhappy squad, too—doing all these against their natural inclinations—and as a poor substitute for the exercise which common sense ought to have dictated from their earliest years.

And half the time ruddy-cheeked boys with hot health exuding from every pore would pause in their outdoor game of bat and ball, come and gaze in at the hermetically-sealed windows where we were playing these awkward pranks, and laugh at us.

A half-hour's romping in the open air is worth more than all the calisthenics in the books, to a girl with any life at all in her.

Nevertheless I earnestly recommend calisthenics (as better than no exercise at all) for those poor skeletons of sickly women whose constitutions are ruined, whose backs are in a chronic state of aching as miserably as if they'd been hoeing a potato field, who feel a never-ending "bearing down," and are finally borne down—and then, please God, borne up!

A sickly woman may perhaps be a healthy angel; for that let us ever pray.

XXVI.

WELL, my lady is home from school. She has left girlhood behind her. What has she got in exchange? You have spent hundreds of dollars on her, fretted about her, deprived yourself of her society, and what return does she make for all this? Put your affection aside, weigh her in the balance of true womanhood, what is her worth?

Is she strong?—strong in body, mind, heart, soul? Or is she a complaining creature with a white face, who has to lie down for half a day every time she takes an hour's walk; her character as colorless as her cheeks; her education superficial to the last degree; forgetting already the very things she had at the tip of her tongue last week; unable to play the simplest piece on the piano "without her notes;" her mind as unformed as when she was a dozen years old; her past a record of woman-teasing; her future an expectant record of man-teasing. No high ambitions, no set career, no bright hopes, nothing to look forward to but a round of eating, drinking, sleeping, shopping, flirting and a husband.

Mrs. Peruser, do not get angry at your daughter if haply you should find her made on this pattern. It is more your fault than hers. Why, with splendid material, did you cut this creature so narrow, shorten the front breadths of her soul, hump up into an enormous pannier the gross organs of her self-conceit, her vanity, her love of wealth? No wonder she is the deformity she is.

I read the other day an interesting recital by a lady who had travelled extensively in China. We are wont to look upon the condition of women in that country as something too pitiable; yet this lady gave it as her frank opinion that the same general code of laws for women prevailed there as here. Women are kept helpless and pretty because it pleases men; poor parents make agonizing and humiliating sacrifices in order to make their daughters "small-feet" women, because that is an attractive feature to men—even as poor parents here struggle to give their daughters fine clothes, have them taught attractive accomplishments, for the obvious—often confessed—purpose of catching a husband.

Come now, mother and father, why not leave this husband out of the question—as completely as you leave the wife out of the question in your boy's case? Suppose your girl has a taste for literature: why not foster that taste? Why not in all your conversation with her let her see that your mind is full of her future great career? Why not speak of it thus: "We expect you to be a great authoress, my dear. Give your whole mind to it. We will set you on the road to fame and fortune as fairly as we can. We believe in your talent—and we believe the world too will one day believe in it."

I take literature as an illustration merely because it is handy; the literary road is wider for woman now than it once was; the entrance to it is easier; so easy, in fact, that there is now some jostling among the eager. But, suppose your daughter has other tastes—no more strange now than literature once was—suppose she wishes to be a great traveller. Shall you crush this wish out of her breast, clip her wings, spend the money which would have gratified her desire on flaunting finery and say, "Sit down now, and suck your thumbs in the approved womanly manner until you catch a husband?"

Do you ask, How can a woman travel alone? That is mere stay-at-home ignorance. Thousands of women cross the ocean alone, yearly. Madame Ida Pfeiffer went twice around the world alone, penetrating into the interior of Africa and of Asia among savage tribes. The lady to whom I referred just now went to China and back alone. Other women, too, have made the circuit of the globe, travelling without male escort. You may have noticed that bright rosy-cheeked girl who walks daily with brisk footsteps in Central Park—sometimes in the morning, sometimes in the afternoon, but daily in all weathers. That girl has been all alone to India. Some wiseacres remonstrated with the friends with whom she lives (she is an orphan) on the impropriety of so pretty a girl walking in a public place like the Central Park unattended by cavalier, matron or servant. They thought it right to be suggested to her that she should have some escort.

"What an insult so paltry a suggestion would be," was the sensible reply, "to a splendid girl who has had sufficient courage and self-reliance to make the voyage to India alone!"

Suppose your daughter should desire to keep a store? Why not set her up in one? Can't afford it? You afford it for your son. It would wound your pride? Ah, there's the wretched old pinching shoe! How I abominate it!

Why can't you be brave, be advanced, conquer this old-time habit of petty thought, show your neighbors how much more progressive and large-minded you are than they? Instead of being ashamed of it, be proud of it. Have her name painted on a signboard in letters a foot high, and let everybody *see* that you rejoice in your daughter's wide-awake, nineteenth-century spirit.

And then see, too, how changed would be the demeanor of the young men of her acquaintance—those self-glorifying individuals who think every woman who looks at them once is in love with them; veritable sultans who imagine they have only to fling down their handkerchiefs, and every girl in the town will scramble for the honor of picking it up. Every community is full of these noble types of adolescent manhood. I know certainly a million specimens "of my own knowledge." Their governing idea is that most girls are fools and ninnies—fit for nothing but playthings; and when they meet one who is not of this character, one with whom they cannot play the fool, then they dub her strong-minded, a horrible new-fangled-idead creature, masculine, and what not.

But they respect her!

Believe me, good parent, that the knowledge that she is of some importance in the world, is going to have a career, to make her mark, will fill your daughter with renewed energy; it will take that pain out of her back like magic; put fire in her eyes; color in her cheeks.

I have known what it is to be an enforced dawdler around the house, without any outlet for what energy and ability I possessed; eating the bread of idleness and dependence, sleeping the sleep of the sluggard, living the life of the do-nothing, yawning, listless *ennuyée.* And I have known what it is to have an OBJECT put in my life, sending the blood coursing like a torrent through my veins, arousing my best energies and my earnest determination to show those who loved me what I could do—and what I did. I had as many back-aches as your daughter, Mrs. Peruser, in the old times. I'm better now, thank you.

It may strike you that not all women would say Amen! to the voice that announced to them that there was a career open to them in which they might go battle and struggle as their brothers do for a livelihood. And in conceding that this is the case I cannot refrain from asking whose fault it is? Is it the fault of this human creature whom God has endowed with brains and heart the same as her brothers? Can you conceive that if this girl of twenty had been reared in a society where absolutely no prejudicial pressure was brought to bear to bias her judgment and influence her verdict she would elect to live an aimless life, to die after years of idleness leaving no more mark of her having lived than the sparrows do when they fall? I warrant me, no; there is no greater love of idleness, no more leaning toward nonentity, in my sex than there is in yours, dear sir.

XXVII.

THE French system of business partnerships between husband and wife is an excellent one on many accounts. Girls are encouraged, in their efforts to make themselves a career, by the knowledge that they are not interfering with their chances for making a happy marriage by so doing. Quite the reverse.

And I admit—and nowhere in this book will you find anything looking to a different opinion—that a happy marriage is a thing to which all good girls everywhere do and always will look forward hopefully, as to a bright spot in the future.

All I have said about leaving girls free to choose their career as boys are left free—about teaching girls to earn their own livelihood as boys are taught—about encouraging girls to the idea of independence as a boy is encouraged—will be sharply misconstrued by my reader if he does not see that my aim is, after all, to glorify MARRIAGE.

I would rob marriage of the curses which cling to it, like barnacles to a noble ship.

I would lift marriage out of the mire of the market-place, where now women scramble for it with unseemly and indecent haste.

I would hedge it about with more difficulties at the outset, so as to prevent the happening of that fatal malady, whose cure is sought in the keen knife of divorce.

I would make marriage the earthly symbol of Heaven, as it was when God ordained it.

But, while I admire the French for many sensible customs, their custom as regards courtship between young people is not one of those I applaud.

I remember my astonishment at a little incident which passed under my eyes, some years ago in Paris. An American lady friend of mine was to give a grand dinner on the occasion of her birthday. Some of her French acquaintances were invited.

One afternoon when I was calling on my friend, the name of a French Countess was announced. After salutations she said, "I came here to-day principally to ask you a question—is the young Baron de Luynes to be at your dinner?"

"Yes," answered the American lady.

"Then," said the Countess, "you must not feel hurt if I do not bring my daughter Victorine."

"Why, Madame la Comtesse," said the American lady, "Monsieur de Luynes is a charming young man."

"True, true! A very charming young man—far too charming to throw any young girl in contact with. He is poor and in the army. I wish my daughter to marry a man of equal fortune with herself, and one who is not a soldier."

When the Countess took her leave I said to my friend, "Do you not think she was looking rather too far ahead? There is a good wide difference between meeting a gentleman at a dinner party and marrying him."

"That is the way with the French," she

answered; "they never expose their children to the temptation of falling in love with a person whom they might not marry."

Another time I saw this feeling exemplified the other way—by a man refusing to place himself in a similar position. An elderly French lady of my acquaintance had a gentleman friend who wanted to marry. He had a small income—just enough to support himself—and he desired to find a wife with at *least* the same income. A lady with whom I was also acquainted—and it is rather amusing to know that she was an American lady—intimated to the French lady that she would like to meet the gentleman. Her income was nothing like what he required, but she thought if he saw her he would be so pleased with her that he would overlook that. (You know what a mania there is among American women abroad to marry Frenchmen of quality.) But he declined positively to meet her. All the representations concerning her being a delightful person only made him more firm in his resolve. If she was indeed so charming, he explained to his elderly friend, he should certainly become enamored of her; and that would be a fatal mistake. The woman he should marry *must* have a certain income. Otherwise he could not marry. He would not marry even such a woman if she did not please him; but the income must be there in the first place. Then they'd see about pleasing each other afterwards.

A French engaged couple are never allowed to be one instant alone together before marriage. The low standard of morality among men, and the entire absence of knowledge of the world in which girls are kept, make French parents feel this to be necessary. I suppose they do for the best according to the circumstances which surround them; but this is a poor way for young people to find out anything about each other's character. I am so far from advocating this policy for American girls, that I think a young girl and a young man, even without being engaged, should be allowed at least little snatches of conversation entirely undisturbed by the presence of another party. What is the use of inviting a young man to come and call on your daughter, and then

making your daughter sit off in a corner mum-chance while you—old father, or prim mother—monopolize all the conversation with the young man yourself? He didn't come here to pay his addresses to you; and it may happen to you to wake up to the knowledge that the young man finds it dull calling at your house, and being obliged to entertain old folks instead of doing some honest courting to your daughter; and he perhaps comes to the conclusion that your daughter isn't half so clever or so lively as your neighbor's daughter, who is allowed to see him for half an hour alone before the old folks come down, and perhaps a little five minutes in the entry-way at parting.

XXVIII.

If ever a duty was clearly marked out for a parent it is this: to see to it that his pure daughter shall be mated to no impure man. And it is rather late in the day to set about testing the condition of his morals when a young man has been visiting at your house for months, and your daughter is hopelessly infatuated with him. It is because the stern parent has developed his sternness so stupidly and neglectfully late in the day, that we so often find children and parents in conflicting attitudes, and grievous wrong resulting for both.

I do not believe there is a father walking this earth who desires other than her own happiness for his daughter; but fathers are so often too careless or too busy to note what acquaintances their daughters make! And so they jog along with eyes blinded to danger until they find enthroned a power of authority in the shape of a young man who three months ago was a stranger to them all, but who now wields an influence stronger than the parents' own.

I knew a girl who married a drunkard—oh, but one of those beastly drunkards who drop into gutters and are dragged home at night by indignant but sympathizing friends, or who lie down on dramshop lounges and sleep until they are pitched out doors by the proprietors. All this at night, you understand. In the daytime he was bright enough, and very fascinating in his ways. He began visiting at the girl's father's house along with a lot of other young men, and her father neither thought nor said nor knew much about him. Suddenly came the astounding announcement to the father that his daughter wished to marry this young man—*would* marry him—or die in the attempt. *Then* this tardy father set to work to learn something about the character of the young man who wished to take from him the young soul who during long years—all the years of her life—had been so tenderly reared, so earnestly prayed for, so nearly idolized; and then he found out that this proposed husband into whose care he was asked to surrender his pure treasure, was the beastly drunkard I have shown. And what do you suppose happened when he told her? Why, she called him a *liar!* Yes, her grayhaired father, whose authority she had never before disputed, whose love for her she had never before dreamed of doubting—she turned upon him with flashing eyes and bitter taunts, and said he was a *liar*, and that he wished to break her heart. And less than a week after, she had eloped with the man who encouraged her to believe that her father was a liar, and swore to her that he had never touched a drop of ardent spirits in his life. The very night of their marriage he reeled into the room of the hotel where they were stopping—and in which they had been married about three hours before—so drunk that he had forgotten everything that had happened, and was perfectly astounded to find her in his bedroom; and even turned upon her in his drunken rage and called her an immodest girl, and bade her go home to her father.

She went—you may imagine how heartbroken. Her father's arms were open.

"But my darling," he said, "I told you this."

"Yes, dear father, I know you did," she said, sobbing and hiding her head on his breast, "but I loved him and I could not believe it. Oh, why didn't you find out something about him before he had robbed me of my heart!"

Herein you will perhaps see illustrated what virtue there is in the French plan which allows no acquaintanceship between ineligible young people.

Any gentleman who habitually visits a young

lady ought to be so perfectly well known to the family of that young lady that if he should propose to-morrow, the only question need be, "Do you love each other sufficiently?" Everything else ought to have been understood as satisfactory long ago; and if all was not satisfactory, no acquaintanceship should have been allowed.

"Victorine may not see Monsieur de Luynes at your dinner table," said Madame la Comtesse, "because he is not eligible as a husband. He is charming, and she is young. Dangerous attributes! No, no! She must find her lover and husband among the *eligible* acquaintances by whom I shall surround her."

Eligibility may mean with the Countess money and position simply; with us it can be made to mean good character, pure morals, religious excellence. Surround your daughter with these, and let her make her heart-choice from among a group of men so excellent that love alone shall settle the question as to which of her admirers she will marry.

Then, with God's blessing on them, let them

freely exchange their tender ideas and heart-longings undisturbed. You needn't sit like a cat watching a mouse—or two mice. You have reared your daughter with laxity indeed if you cannot trust to her self-protecting sense of honor now. You must have small faith in the man to whom you are willing to intrust this precious soul which God put into your hands to care for, if you have not also confidence in him. Let him pay his addresses to her undisturbed; let him say the sweet little foolish things which stir her heart so deeply, but which might stir your risibles; let him sing his love-songs to her and request her to meet him by moonlight alone (*alone*, you observe!) with such expression as *love* gives the human voice, without your standing by in grim judgment on his performances, as if he were an opera-singer, and had charged you something for listening to him.

Those blissful hours of courtship! Are they ever forgotten?—the hand-pressure at the gate; the strolls under the elm-trees; the snatched kiss under the umbrella on that terrible rainy night, you know. Gracious! Don't I pity the married couple who can't look back on such sweet, fond, foolish pictures as this, in memory's magic picture-book!

Husband, where is that poem about "Making Memories," which you wrote when we were at the seaside that summer?

Ah, here it is:

MAKING MEMORIES.

Making beautiful memories
  To sweeten our lives in another day;
To be remembered in the years
  Waiting for us in the far away.

Leafy groves, where long, cool shades
  Woo unto rambling hour on hour;
To be remembered like a dream—
  Leaf and bird and grass and flower.

Under the white moonlight last night
  Where we whispered, hand in hand,
Looking out from the pillar's shade
  Over the beach with its white, white sand—

There was a picture! The far-off stars,
  The near-by daisies, the sighing sea;
The good-night pressure of hands; the words
  That fluttered down from your window to me.

The commonest thing of our to-day
  Will sometime be a poem, a dream;

Bathed in the light of the far away,
 How fair, how fair, these hours will seem!

Much of this is for memories—
 Much perhaps will be forgot;
But the word that told me you loved me, love,
 Oh, that will not! oh, that will not!

"A thing of that sort is rather pleasanter to remember than it was to experience," says husband, lighting a cigar; "and it wasn't unpleasant to experience, either."

I am acquainted with a couple in the South who have been married twenty-one years! Twenty-one years! What changes have happened since these two were romantic lovers and were enjoying their blissful courtship! Nine beings—nine human souls—have entered their world and their love since then. And their love has grown like compound interest, for each of these nine is loved as much as the originals themselves, and the originals love each other nine or ninety times more than then.

I visited them recently in their southern home. Though it was early spring by the calendar, the warmth of summer had already reached their climate; and it was pleasant to sit in their pretty though plain parlor, with the windows open, and the odor of South-blooming flowers scenting the air. Soon the moon arose with that mellow radiance, that rich golden hue peculiar to the South, and the husband stepped out on the balcony. All was still. He leaned through the window and said softly, "Dora, come out and look at the moonlight."

Then it was a sight to see that serene and stout mother of nine children and one at the breast—(he was there at the precise moment I am speaking of, too)—hurry out with all the romance of a girl of sixteen to look at the moonlight. He put his arm about her thick waist. "Just twenty-one years ago to-night," he said, "we were married."

The stillness was kept so sacred and profound by those within the room, that we could hear the unromantic little rogue—number nine—voicing his content with murmurous lips, as the three stood there where the moonlight shed its rich beams upon them.

"It was just such a night as this," said she, "that we roamed about Niagara, where we went on our wedding tour. Oh, wasn't that a blissful time?"

"Not more so than this," he answered, and kissed her as tenderly as he did then, I'll be bound.

Ah, how we admired that romantic couple of forty-five or so, as we sat within and listened! Surely, surely, there is nothing on earth so beautiful as wedded love.

My friends' house was burned during the war—all the loved accumulations of years destroyed in an hour by a victorious general's torch. That was hard, wasn't it? I think so. We mingle our tears, talking of the war. We were on different sides, you know—but what of that? What is a political issue—what are fifty political issues—compared to a tried and true friendship of long years' duration?—at least when the political issue is dead, and the friendship lives. "If secession was a sin," they say, "we have dearly paid for it." And they have. If all sins were so terribly avenged, we should all of us perhaps be more virtuous—or less. Meantime they are now, as they were before the war, our brothers; our dashing, handsome, generous, warm-hearted Southern brothers; and the girls are our lovely, dark-eyed, romantic Southern sisters, who used to be the heroines of the novels for their beauty's sake, and the men the heroes for their impetuous sense of honor, their rash bravery, their open-handed generosity.

Shame upon those writers North and South who have so distorted character with their venomous pens that the worst, the lowest, the meanest, the most exaggerated type of each section is paraded before the other as a sample of the whole! By these writers of the South, the Freelove woman of New York is held up as the type of Northern womanhood—by these writers of the North, the brutal Legree and the degraded "low-downer" are held up as types of Southern gentlemen. Southern gentlemen! Why, this Philip—this man who has been married twenty-one years, and of whom I have been speaking—he is a Southern gentleman. Find me a grander!

XXIX.

I PITY the young man who has to pay his addresses at a house where there are several sisters. He stands such a strong chance of being unmercifully ridiculed by the sisters he is not in love with. They, being only lookers-on, can calmly criticise everything about him. The merry rogues burst with laughter at every sign of his lovesickness, and lie awake giggling after they have gone to bed, at the remembrance of the sigh he heaved when he was leaving, and how funny he looked when he cast up his eyes in his love-throes.

Then of course the sister whom he fancies, wishes to know what "the girls" think of him; and without the slightest malice the fun-loving monkeys pronounce him "Pretty nice, but rather countrified," and tell Lillie when she marries him she really must not let him sing his hymns through his nose. And there! The first you know, ridicule from those absurd little girl-critics, her sisters, has killed the incipient fondness that was in Lillie's breast, and the poor fellow gets the mitten.

Don't do it, girls! If Sister has a beau, retire discreetly to the background; don't hear nor see what he says and does. Many things in him that seem very absurd to you are very sweet in her eyes; and would remain so if you didn't bring to bear the weight of your trifling judgment on it, and so change admiration into a sense of her beau's being a laughing-stock—which no girl can stand.

Just think how you would feel, Miss Laughing-Eyes, if Charley Goodboy were to bring his brothers with him when he comes to pay his addresses to you, and you were forced to play the agreeable while you knew your every action was under sharp criticism—and the criticism of ridicule—from the young gentlemen. But the parallel to this has more than once come to my knowledge.

I knew a household where there were four sisters—four sweet, happy, pretty, healthy girls. They were extremely attached to each other, this Fanny, Libbie, Ursula (alias Puss) and Mamie. I suppose they never had in all their lives a secret from each other, and each thought that the three others were the three most splendid girls that ever trod the earth.

There wasn't one atom of selfishness in these girls. They were rather a large party, you see, and it wasn't always convenient to take all of them out pleasuring at once; for instance, in any ordinary carriage, the four girls filled it, and there wasn't room for anybody else; so their all going at once wasn't to be thought of; and then came the scramble as to *who* should go. Each became stricken with the determination to stay at home, so that the others might have the enjoyment.

"Now Mamie, you shall go! You didn't go last time—go, darling!"

"No, deary—you go; I'd rather you and Puss should go. It'll do you good."

"Well, I won't go, that's flat! Fannie needs a drive more than I do."

So these dear little self-abnegating darlings would go on until you became almost as exasperated as if they were disputing selfishly instead of generously. One day last winter their father, who writes for the papers, got two tickets for Nilsson sent him, and he could only take *one* of the girls. Goodness gracious! What a maddening, self-sacrificing time they did have about that! Their father got angry at last, and said He'd be hanged if any of them should go; he'd burn the ticket up, or take Aunt Polly, who is as deaf as a post, and nearly blind into the bargain.

It's just the same way about the girls' clothing. If one gets something new, the first thing she does is to go steal her arm around the waist or neck of one of her sisters, and try to relinquish the new finery. Anything really fresh and pretty goes a begging, for all are too unselfish to appropriate it. After it's faded perhaps they come to an understanding, and agree to wear it by turns. Thus sashes, neck-ribbons, collars, slippers, rings, brooches and sleeve-buttons belong to this commonwealth of four members.

They have solved many a Utopian scheme; their very wardrobe is coöperative. Eight willing hands accomplish household labors in a jiffy. They draw lots for the sweeping, and the one who gets it is triumphant, and the three others fret because they fear it is too hard for her. Finally I may say that you can't please Fannie half so much any other way as you can by "raving" over the accomplishments of Libbie, Puss, and Mamie; and to gain the hearts of Mamie, Puss, and Libbie you have only to sing the praises of their sister Fan.

Of course they have long ago settled what sort of man they are going to marry. This would be all very well except that the kind of man they have fixed on don't exist. This, you will confess, is a drawback; but if their beau ideal did exist, I pity the poor fellow if he should come along and there should be only one of him! What a scrambling there would be on the part of the four self-sacrificers to present him each to the other! He'd have to submit to a worse fate than Solomon's baby. (On second thought it was not Solomon's baby, but only a baby he threatened to halve.)

The kind of man the four girls had settled to marry (a long time before Bob Stevens fell in love with Fan) was just twenty-one and a half years old; six feet high; so straight he leaned the other way; fall in his back; small feet done up in tight patent-leather boots; complexion of marble whiteness; nose straight on a line with his forehead, like the nose of a Grecian statue; deep, large, blue eyes; black hair curling all over his head; long, silky, black moustache, excruciatingly waxed at the ends; ruby-red lips, and teeth as regular as the false sets in the dentist's show-case. His conversation was to be one stream of poetical quotation; and he was to bow half-way to the ground every time he encountered the sisters, without in the least disturbing the fall of his trouser-leg over his instep. He was to be a poet, a scholar, and a philosopher; he was to sing like Mario and waltz like Taglioni; and rich—oh, the Count of Monte Cristo or old Crœsus himself shouldn't be richer!

And that isn't half.

Meantime, here was plain Robert Stevens desperately in love with Fan!

Poor Bob! He couldn't keep away. Every evening during the soft summer when his fondness for Fan first developed itself, he would walk timidly up to the girls' doorstep after supper, and face the whole four of them, and say, "Good evening, Miss Fannie. Hope I see you well."

How that Puss and Mamie did have this phrase over and over! Little rascals, they slept two in a bed and all four in one large room, and before Fan got her eyes open in the morning they would hop out in their night-clothes, and go and half smother her with kisses and shout in her ear "Good morning, Miss Fannie. Hope I see you well."

"Oh, don't tease me so, girls, don't!" poor Fan would say; "I don't care for him—I don't indeed."

Meantime every day Fannie was feeling the influence of a sweet and strong nature which was pouring out its wealth of adoration at her feet. How she wished the girls would think him "nice!" How she would have enjoyed loving him if those teases had only let her!

"Fully recognizing that his moral character is irreproachable, Fan," said Libbie, "it yet cannot be concealed that his hands are beety—undeniably, manifestly, incontrovertibly, outrageously, not-to-be-stoodably beety."

"'Tis true, 'tis pity, and pity 'tis, 'tis true,"

said Puss, who was reading up Shakespeare in a great hurry so as to be ready for that beau-ideal of a beau who was going to come along so soon.

"Why girls, are they so *very red?*" gasped poor Fan; "I'm not—in love—with him, you know—but really I didn't notice that they were so *very* red!"

"Beets are the only simile," said the merciless Libbie.

As the evenings grew cool in the autumn, Robert had to be asked into the parlor. One night the three tormentors got him to sing. Fannie was on pins and needles, but he thought *she* wanted him to sing and sing he did. Now, Robert had a sweet voice and there was nothing ludicrous about his singing. But you can find spots on the sun if you are determined to look for them.

He'd no sooner gone than the three girls made a dive at the piano.

"When other leaps and otherer hearts"—

"Oh, Libbie, he didn't sing it in that way!" groaned Fannie, laughing in spite of herself.

"Then you'll rememberher *me!*"

"Flat me—awfully nasal me—the *mi* so flat it's a *re*," corrected Mamie.

The result of all this was inevitable. Love could not grow in such an atmosphere. Fannie began to avoid him. Robert was in truth a young man of keen perceptions and great power of will, and he perceived her aim and quietly withdrew from a suit which was not agreeable.

Fannie didn't mean quite so much as that. In fact she didn't mean anything—except that she didn't like to be laughed at quite so much; that was all.

Two years after—and the beau-ideal was as far from making his appearance as ever—Robert Stevens's wedding-cards, elegantly engraved, came to hand. He hadn't seemed ludicrous in the eyes of the richest, as well as one of the handsomest and most refined girls in town. In fact, Fan and her sisters looked up to Miss Beaumont much as a family of darling, cunning, frisky little King Charles spaniels might look up to a tall, slender, aristocratic and altogether superb Italian greyhound. And

Robert had won Miss Beaumont's hand and heart.

Fan and the three other girls went to the wedding. The church was crowded and they had to stand right out at the door; almost on the very steps. When the ceremony was over, and Robert came out with his bride on his arm ("White satin and real point," whispered Libbie) he lifted his hat politely, and bowing quite low ("his trouser-legs perfectly undisturbed over his instep," said Puss afterwards) he looked Fan straight in the eye and said, "Good evening, Miss Fanny. Hope I see you well!"

XXX.

YOU will say that this little story implies the existence of a sort of love which needs the fostering approbation of others to insure its growth and health. Do you feel scorn for such love as this?—say it is unworthy the name?—merits contempt? Consider conditions.

A girl is reared in a state of absolute dependence on others. She has—as people call it—

"no mind of her own." They mean by this that she has never been taught to use the mind which she undoubtedly has, and the implication of lack of mind in her would be resented heartily enough, if it were couched in other than the ambiguous phraseology of these cant expressions which mean everything and nothing, and all shades between, as he who utters chooses.

I know a girl—and her case is by no means a rare one—who never bought a pair of shoes for herself until after she was twenty years of age. Flanked—like the girls I have just mentioned—by loving sisters, mother, and sometimes also by cousins and friends, she would proceed to the shoe-shop, and after the merits of the leather, the sewing, the cut, the finish, and the fit of the different samples had been judged by the assembly, she would find herself the possessor of the necessary shoes. You will not laugh when I tell you that it was a real trial to this girl when—after her marriage, and when far away from her family—she found herself put to the terrible ordeal of choosing for herself a pair of shoes. She was, indeed, very much distressed about it.

"I don't know whether they fit me or not!" she whimpered (when the shoemaker asked, "How does *them* do?"), "and I don't know whether you're cheating me or not. I don't know whether shoes ought to cost one dollar or twenty."

Which confession of ignorance was equalled by a young housekeeper who said to me confidentially, "I positively don't know whether a pound of butter is as big as a cheese or as small as an egg; but I don't think the servants suspect. I always look so wise and shake my head so disapprovingly at everything."

Gussie and I went to church together, the other day, to hear a young Congregationalist minister. I love the Congregationalist service —so simple, so earnest, so hearty. No offense to those dear brothers and sisters who are not Congregationalists, but there is something about the unassuming simplicity of this service which wins me more than most others. However, that is not the point. The point is, that I was charmed with this young minister's sermon; so fresh, so soulful, so honest. I thank you for the good it did me, young reverend, here on my printed page. Gussie asked me how I liked it when we left the church. I told her I was charmed—was not she?

"Y-e-s,—yes."

And then the minister—so young, so honest, so evidently pure-hearted—was *he* not one to be admired?

"Y-e-s" again—yes; but there was a mental reservation; truthful little Gussie could not conceal that from my prying eyes. By and by out it came. Did I not think he had Rather a Big Chin?

Was I surprised? A little. Did I laugh? No. Did I treat this curious criticism with grand contempt—superior scorn? Not at all. I know the girl-heart and the girl-mind too well. Besides, I love Gussie dearly, and I consider her a girl of keen intelligence; but she has not lived so many years as I; and perhaps she has a girlish beau-ideal of an impossibly beautiful man, like the four sisters of the preceding chapter—a beau-ideal by which she tries even her ministers on occasion, as well as her beaux. I granted the undeniable fact that the young minister had Rather a Big Chin—in fact, Quite a Big Chin. What then? Why, that was so much in his favor! I cited all the Big Chins of history—brought up a long line of distinguished Big Chins, and finally concluded my preach with an eloquent peroration on the strength, power, bull-dog perseverance and thorough value of a well-directed and religious-minded Big Chin. And Gussie saw that and other Big Chins thenceforth with new, and approving, eyes.

Now, what I mean to urge regarding girls in general is, that their judgment—even the judgment of the bright, intelligent, quick-witted and discerning among them—is, after all, the callow judgment of *youth*. And being such, it is likely to trip on some contemptibly insignificant matter like this of chins, and fall into errors that are simply appalling to think of.

If there is anything more absurd in all modern civilization than the practice of setting callow girls and green boys to passing judgment on their fellow-creatures of the opposite sex, with a view to the gravest relations of life, I cannot imagine what it is.

It is to me one of the best possible auguries for the future of a young girl, that she is anxious others should smile upon and approve her love. In itself, it is a promise of womanly wisdom most cheering to behold. But, like many another good thing, it needs the right sort of treatment, if it is to yield good fruit. A peach-tree is a good thing, but it will bear no fruit if it be not properly tended. The very best qualities in girls are often wasted—die without so much as a blossom, much less fruit—simply from want of that sort of care which the good gardener gives the flower and the good parent the child. The good gardener does not try to twist the graceful lily into a climbing vine; he does not seek to make violets grow on rose-bushes. All his aim is, to *train* the plant, and help it to grow in that direction *which is natural to it.*

When parents realize that herein—and herein alone—lies *their* office, they will not do violence to their daughters' hearts in anything. They will know how to deal with love.

XXXI.

I RATHER favor the "stern parent," myself.

It is a delicate matter to assail old traditions in sentimental literature. People rebel so indignantly at anything which seems to lay disrespectful hands on their sentimental idols.

I have seen daggers looking from the eyes of painfully young persons when, in speaking to audiences, I have assailed the favorite old romantic situations of the story-tellers in respect to the fond heroine who loves the penniless hero, and wants to live on moonshine instead of beefsteak.

"It is not so much the man," says the handsome Bella Wilfer, in *Our Mutual Friend*, "as the establishment."

It has been the custom of novelists from time immemorial to hold up to scorn and obloquy the base creature who marries for an establishment, and to exalt to the seventh heaven of heroinism the young lady who marries for love.

The "stern parent," who, having been through years enough of life to have learned common sense, wishes to assure his daughter's future comfort, according to existing states of society—the father with some practical knowledge of the cost of bread and butter, and the shiftlessness of the average young man, becomes a sharer in the obloquy which falls upon the "mercenary."

But I shudder to think of the state of things we should presently have on our hands if the common-sense papas were all to die off suddenly, and leave the girls free to rush headlong into "love-matches."

Sufficient to the generation is the evil thereof. It is a blessing that so many papas remain to act as balance-wheels to the disjointed machinery of youthful passion.

Do I then advocate the marrying for an establishment?

I no more advocate marrying for an establishment than I advocate marrying for fun.

Marrying for fun is, however so very popular among the story-tellers that, for a change, I should not object to reading a story in which the heroine should have brains in her head as well as love—so called—in her heart. At any rate, I should like to have real-life girls act as if they were made on that pattern ; and before consenting to marry the adorable Charlie or Billy or Josiah, find out whether the young man is equal to the requirements of a weekly board-bill for two, with a prospect of more. If it should be carried to the extent of finding out whether the adorable Charlie or Billy or Josiah could pay house-rent and market bills, and the divers sundries which are involved in "keeping house," I should not look upon it as altogether heinous.

I cannot frown upon any human being who seeks to escape from the typical boarding-house —that hotbed of scandals and iniquities whose inventor deserves Sancho Panza's blessing—*inverted.*

So long as society is arranged in such a manner that the man is the bread-winner and woman's chief duty is to take care of his babies and keep his house in order, it ought to be a by-law of the system that no girl shall enter upon wedlock until she sees the house she has to keep as well as the man she is to keep it for.

But if you think because I say this that I am

in favor of that common crime known as "marrying for money," you are greatly mistaken.

The woman who dares to put her heart out of the question, and without a thought of love to sell herself to a man whose material wealth she desires to share is—to put it mildly—a trafficker. That she responds in the proper places in the marriage-service, holding the hand of the man to whom she gives her body, but who has no place in her heart—that she is in the eye of the law henceforth his wife—*that* does not help her. In the eye of God she is no more his wife than I am.

I knew one such woman——

Do not, whatever you do, fall into the mistake of supposing that I do not know dozens of such women—for I do, and so do you, and so do we all.

I knew one such woman, who married a man she did not love, but whose money she wanted to finger. She would have recoiled in horror from the intimation that she bartered away her chastity by the act. She was young, beautiful, well-bred, and no more inclined to sin than the rest of us.

Soon after her marriage her husband went into Wall Street and made kites of his money. Soon after that he took to the flowing bowl for consolation. Every night he came home to dinner completely bowled over.

And presently his wife found out that her life was unbearable and that she hated the drunken lout to whom she was tied for life. His money was gone, and with it all was gone which made him tolerable to her. She had taken a man for the sake of an "establishment" in the sense commonly understood. And when she ran away one day last spring with a penniless young dandy whom she had met at their common boarding-house, she fancied she had now taken a man for his own sake.

He had excited "pleasing sensations" in her discontented breast, and so—for the second time—she had outraged wifehood by taking a man without the marriage of Heaven.

(Webster, you know, defines the verb to love as "to regard with affection on account of some qualities which excite pleasing sensations.")

What then are we to marry for, if not for love nor for an establishment? These are the two incitements to marriage.

Je veux bien. Nobody denies that.

You are to marry—if you will pardon my speaking in a manner somewhat *ex cathedra*—for True Love, and for nothing else whatever. But you are to use at least as good a judgment in the matter as that which a business man uses in investing his capital—or—you are to take the consequences.

You are to treat your love as the precious soul-capital of your life, and you are no more to venture it in rash and unconsidered speculations than a wise business man ventures his money in such a way. He studies the matter carefully. Do you at least as much. Sometimes he fails in spite of all. So may you. But then it is your misfortune, not your fault; and you will bear failure better, in this case, if you are a true-hearted woman.

If Scylla and Charybdis are pointed out to you, you can at least try to avoid wrecking yourself upon them.

What is wanted on the one hand is a genuine sense of VIRTUE, to prevent the cold-hearted from converting marriage into legalized sin.

What is wanted on the other hand is COM-

MON SENSE, to prevent the hot-headed from rushing into the fire of passion as moths rush into flame.

Marriage is the holiest and loveliest thing there is in this world. Love is the basis of marriage. And of no one thing in the world we inhabit is so much and such hopeless twaddle written as of this same love.

In spite of my deep respect for Noah Webster I think his definition of love is about as puerile a thing as ever was printed. Love cannot be defined. Nevertheless I see these truths plainly concerning it:

1. That passion, love's counterfeit, is no more love than hunger is.

2. That love does not burn with serene and beautiful flame in the lamp of sordid and unworthy lives.

3. That love does not endure to the end unless it be sustained by *virtue* in the lover and the beloved.

4. And that love will die, just as purity will vanish, just as men will turn from morality to sin, from righteousness to crime, where the causes are sufficient to effect the change.

XXXII.

AFTER all, the thing which seems to me most wonderful in this world is, that truth should be so old! You think you have discovered something new in the way of advanced thought, fresh fancy, progressive idea, when, lo and behold! somebody comes along and tells you the Chinese had it fifteen hundred centuries before Christ. Confucius had it set to music, and Solomon danced a *pas seul* to it on the back-stoop of his Temple.

As many as a hundred times during the progress of this book I have been on the point of scratching out this and that sentence because somebody else said something like that long ago; then I have hesitated, because if I once began with that idea, I felt I might as well scratch the whole book out and be done with it.

After that, to be consistent, I might go and scratch myself out, because I individually have been repeated ever since God made Eve; my hair, my eyes, my nose, my ears, my teeth, have all passed through a most bewildering number of editions; and yet our neighbor Mrs. Perkins had last night a little daughter, and the whole household is as much fluttered and excited about it as if this little daughter were Number One of a new species.

I hate to feel called on to quote that tattered and torn Solomonism which gasps forth every day that there is nothing new under the sun. Yet most emphatically this is thus. There is not a grand thought preached from any pulpit, —there is not a noble line penned on any page, which has not been thought ages ago, which has not been penned long years before any of us were born. You may turn your phrase freshly, you may clothe your idea in quaint neologisms, but the idea has been used before, be sure of it. It has been said—and betted upon (which indicates a stronger certainty with some people)—that there is not a brilliant thought the human mind is capable of thinking which has not been brilliantly thought and well expressed by Shakespeare. I have been familiar with Shakespeare since my earliest girlhood, yet it never struck me that the Bard had said ——. But wait.

We have three birds—gorgeous bits of color, rarely seen here in the North. They are called "Nonpareils" in the South, and they are bright gems of the tropics quite glorious to behold. The man of whom we bought them in Savannah told me to kill flies occasionally and give them to the birds as tit-bits, and they would soon learn to love me and to welcome my approach to their cage. But at the outset I discover that I don't like to kill flies. I recoil at the necessity of winning the affection of the birds by assuming the *rôle* of fly-assassin. I am such a great, powerful monster beside this curious little hop-o'-ty-skip which runs familiarly along my page as I write, that it seems not only cruel but cowardly in me to deliberately smash it, and make mourning in its family, when it is not doing me the least harm. And here is my new idea: Is it not possible that we mortals may be the poor insects scampering about in a seemingly—often really—idiotic manner—building our little monuments, as ants do their hills, only to be kicked over by thoughtless boys; that we are the insignificant hop-o'-ty-skips running along the printed page of some mighty Jove or Jupiter who deliberately smashes us and winds up our career forever? This idea I had thought quite new—really original—and had intended to elaborate it some day in print in a humorous fashion; when husband informed me that it was as old as the hills.

"Old?" I gasped, amazed.

"Why, certainly! the Chinese discovered it fifteen hundred centuries before Christ. Confucius set it to music and Solomon——

"Oh, do stop, Mister Teaze!"

"Well then, behold! look here in Shakespeare:—

> "'As flies to wanton boys, so we to the gods;
> They kill us for their sport.' KING LEAR."

—So now I am more than ever convinced that Solomon was right; and that the truth will bear infinite repetition. It is only error that grows stale, flat, and unprofitable with repeated utterance.

It is a good thing to speak the truth once; it is better to speak it twice; and it is best to speak it all the time. Repetition is only another name for agitation, and if you mean to do any good in this world you must persistently hammer away.

XXXIII.

I REMEMBER when I was a child that I often wondered if all the birds had nests. As if there could be any difficulty about building a nest, with all the countless trees in the forest ready to build in! Yet, who knows what conditions of ornithological social life may trammel and regulate the free action of birds? There are not more trees in the forests than there are twenty-by-one-hundred-foot building lots on the face of the great globe. Yet not every man has a nest. You would think, with the great globe to choose from, that every man would build him a home. The materials for his house are as profuse at hand as those which go to building the birds' nests, are they not? Only labor is required; and that the bird gives. Why not man? Especially when the term of deepest pity, the profoundest word-symbol of an abject, pitiable, and unfriended condition is —"homeless!"

So great an influence is wielded by the home-life, so intimately are love for individuals and love of home blended, that I am almost convinced a law should be passed, that none should marry except on condition that they *go at once into a home of their own.* Not a room, nor a suite of rooms, in a hotel or boarding-house, but a Home—a spot of earth sacred to the household gods, and over whose threshold none may pass but by the permission of the man and wife who dwell together therein.

For there is so much that is softening and soothing—so much that is peaceful, reposeful, restful in the bare idea of a nook which you independently inhabit, that the ruggedest nature cannot but feel it. The fiercest barbarian that ever roamed the woods is more mild, more peaceable in his hut-home. Turn from his comfortable, cheerful home the gentlest man you know—force him to beat about the four corners of the city, now lying in this strange bed, now eating at that uncongenial board, his lares and penates scattered, his familiar surroundings vanished, and in a little time you will not be able to recognize your once amiable man in this soured, petulant, distressed creature who has been so unfortunate as to lose his home.

Hammering away in a moral smithy, I find that sometimes the sparks fly. But the faithful workman does not quit his work, if perchance a spark should light upon his bared arm, and sting. He rubs the spot a moment perhaps, but he goes on hammering presently.

I have been stung on occasion, but I have not on that account struck any the less cordially the moment after.

It has been my plan, since I became in some sense a worker for reform, to note carefully and respectfully all criticisms on me and my work, and to reply to them, directly or indirectly, as occasion would allow. As I do not swing a wooden sword myself, so I like to see the weapons of others sharp and keen, even though they cut me sometimes cruelly. And the keener they are, the truer my respect for an honorable antagonist.

My critics have been numerous and active; they have given me abundant cause to defend myself; and in defending myself I try to hit as hard as they—but I respect their activity, energy, and skill even while I strike—when they are honorable opponents.

There is a paper still feebly published in this city, which assiduously occupied itself for several months in trying to attract my attention, by belching forth column after column of the vilest calumny at me. Many friends wondered why I did not reply to it. Here and now I will tell you why: Not because its arguments were unanswerable; far from it; they were weaker than water—but because in its anxiety to goad me into replying, it descended to falsehood, to scurrility, to indecent disregard of the code of gentility which should be the guide-manual of editors and gentlemen. Taking one of my articles on theatrical indecency for a pretended theme of criticism, it left criticism idle to vilify me personally, to charge me with base motives, and, instead of endeavoring to pick my argument to pieces, trying to find somewhere in my Past a proof that I was a hypocrite now. The imbecility of this course in a professedly critical journal was so idiotic, that had it been *merely* idiotic I should have laughed at it, and given it a good-natured, though contemptuous whack over the shoulders with my sword. But there is sometimes linked to idiocy a species of dia bolic cunning—a treacherous, fiendish, horrible cruelty of intention—which manifests itself in the most disgusting and frightful wickedness. In the instance I am considering, idiocy of critical purpose passed thus into the diabolism which has no hesitation as to its means, so that it may accomplish its ends, and—as with the idiocy of the asylums—in its eagerness to wreak its will, is heedless of the injury it inflicts upon itself.

Seeing this, I put up my sword at once. I would not lower myself so far as to do battle with such an antagonist.

It was evident that this paper believed it could goad me into a reply or into the institution of a libel suit, and that this would attract attention to it, and advertise it. This is an old game with the publishers of unprofitable newspapers, and it has often been a successful one; but it is too transparent ever to deceive me. My lips were at once sealed; and so far as mentioning the name of this journal is concerned, they are sealed forever. I resolved that not one line of advertising should I ever give it, though it charged me and all my family, and every one of my friends, with every crime known to the calendar.

The old gentleman in the fire-red tights, and the red isinglass eyelids—he who is ever finding some mischief still for idle hands to do—is never so well pleased as when he gets hold of one of those writers for the press whose delight it is to rake over the dead leaves of the Past in search of buried misdeeds.

It is a part of the duty of a newspaper, we must admit, to take cognizance in its columns of passing events, and if crimes are perpetrated, or wrongs done, to give an account of them as matters of news, and perhaps comment upon them editorially also.

Thus, if you should go out some fine day and pick somebody's pocket it would be quite right that all the newspapers should chronicle your offense; nor could you complain if the editors should point out to their readers the wickedness of pocket-picking as illustrated by you.

But, on the other hand, if you had picked a pocket ten years ago, and borne the consequences of your offense at the time—and since then had lived a correct life, a life utterly void of offense, or, still better, a life of charity and usefulness, it would then indeed be most cruel and wicked for any newspaper of to-day to entertain its readers with an account of your old offense, so as to give you pain now and perhaps interfere with your present usefulness.

The man who repents—and who follows up repentance with good works, with a life of honorable effort—this man before all others is worthy of our sympathy. We have the testimony of the Bible that such men are the best beloved of Heaven, and that there is more joy in heaven over one sinner that repents, than over many who have never gone astray.

There is an Italian proverb which says: "If the faults of the best and purest of men were written on his forehead, he would pull his cap over his eyes."

I suppose there is no exception to this rule—not one—and has never been since Christ lived.

The person who rakes up some forgotten peccadillo of yours—even some expiated and buried crime—to injure your influence for the right and true, which you are laboring earnestly to manifest in the present, is guilty of a heinous offense. He is laboring in the service of Satan;

his work is that of a Scavenger; and he is without excuse in any honorable soul.

If a man—or let us say a woman—had violated every commandment in the decalogue—if she had been a drunkard and a thief, a liar, a slanderer, and—well yes, even a free-lover—I say that the farther in the past she leaves these offenses, the more worthy she is of the good-will of all true Christian men and women; and the man or journal which seeks to revive the unhappy Past that it may darken the Present, is a graver offender than his victim ever was.

But if this be so, by what terms shall I characterize the fiendishness of the editor who in his anger at the worthy Robinson should go prowling into the Past, trying to discover if in some forgotten grave there lies not some folly or weakness of which some cherished *friend* of Robinson's, or some member of Robinson's family, has been guilty, and coloring the simplest incidents with the hues of Hades, dangles them in Robinson's face with an air of saying, "Do you see that, sir? We fling this in your face! How do you like *this?* What have you to say to *this?* Your grandmother, or your uncle, or your second cousin's husband did this! And what have you to say *now?* Answer us if you can, sir! Aha! Answer us if you can!"

And a skinny Mephistopheles rubs his hands and chuckles in the background.

I have refused to look in the Past of even Mrs. Freelove in search of her record. Her record may be what it may—I hold that her present position before the public is all the public has to deal with.

I lectured last winter at a certain pretty village in New York State, and took occasion in the course of my remarks to pay my attentions to the Satan of free-love in the phrase which forms the title of this book. The next day on the cars there glided up to me a youngish sort of man, dressed in threadbare black, without gloves on his bony hands, with a sandy and befreckled complexion, and great round staring eyes, whose color seemed to match his complexion so perfectly that they may have been red too, for all impression they made to the contrary. At any rate, they were unsheltered by any visible eyelash, and unadorned by any visible eyebrow; and looking at them you wondered if such eyes were not painful to carry about in their wide and blank openness.

As I turned from the window I found this seedy and creeping man standing by my side. He asked me if I were I. And I answered, "Ay." Without further parley he seated himself by my side. My olfactories are very delicate, and he was musty as well as shabby and red.

"I was at—" and his voice was quavering and high and shrill—"your lecter last evenin'. I am just startin' on a lecter tower myself."

In reporting this man's conversation I do not exaggerate, as a fictionist might, for the purpose of heightening the effect of the picture.

The man was a complete surprise to me. Malapropisms are common on the stage and in books, but this was, I think, the only person I ever met who audaciously used certain words which are a little out of the common, and pronounced them in the most outrageously grotesque manner.

"Yes," he continued, giving me the benefit of his plans—and if there is anything more impertinent than for an utter stranger to sit down uninvited beside you when there is plenty of room elsewhere, and begin to talk to you of his projects about himself, which are not of the slightest interest to you, I know not what it is.

"I am startin' on my fust lecter tower. I am goin' to speak on the Cause."

"What cause?" I asked, with a mechanical politeness. Those years I passed in France have ingrained in my nature a certain suavity of manner of which on occasion I would gladly be rid; and which showed itself for a few minutes during this interview in a decently courteous reception of an insolent and offensive person.

"Why, the Cause! Woman! Seffrage! Oh, woman is a slave! She is bound! She shall be free!"

I shrunk from the person as far as the seat would permit, so sincere was the disgust with which the slimy creature inspired me.

"Yes, I'm goin' inter Cernecticut——ter Bridgeport; thar I shall meet the Reverund Miss Atlas Smith Do you know Reverund Atlas Smith?"

I did not. I was looking out of the window. He addressed me again.

"This will be my deebutt as a lecterer."

I turned and stared at this worm. Excuse me, worms; the simile is degrading to you, but our language is faulty in some respects, and a linguistic peculiarity alone the cause of this insult which likens a most offensive and immoral creature to a harmless and inoffensive little thing like yourselves.

"I hev an exception to take to your lecter," said the worm, rubbing his knuckly hand on his hard, rasping chin, through the skin of which a stubble of red beard was trying to push its way. "You objected to the ductrines of Sister Freelove!"

I began to feel a dawning sense of relief. He went on.

"The ductrines of Sister Freelove I know is not pop'ler—people is agin 'em ginerally. I em a lawyer here in our town, and represuntations was made to me which—which in fact indooced me to espouse the cause of Sister Freelove—and I felt called on to pernounce my protest agin the views you took in your lecter last night."

"You are too kind, sir. I am deeply obliged to you. It is a pleasure, sir, to receive your protest."

"Be keerful!" said he, and his red face grew redder, and his hair grew stiffer, and his bony hand scraped his bony chin more nervously than before; "thar will be a day of reckonin' fer them who set theirselves up agin Sister Freelove. She has got the most extrawd'nary mind of any woman livin', and she is agoin' to occupy a powerful pusition and she will remember her friends. So we air bound to rally round her. She is abreakin' the way fer future generations. Them thet is not with us is aginst us, and we shell use the weepins of defense. You will hev to change your tone if you expect to escape. We shell not allow ourselves to be calumerniated with impunity, mam. I hev heerd all the lecters that hes been given in our town this winter, but none, no none, hes aroused my anermosity ekal to yourn."

"Then for once," I said to him with a flush of real delight, "I am satisfied with myself. I glow with pleasure to think that I have done something that calls for the disapprobation of the low, the vile, the degraded, the creatures who make a boast of their shame. How could I look myself in the face in the glass to-night if I had done something to merit the approval of those who hold *your* doctrines! You have given me a moment of sincere pleasure, Mr. Freelover, and I know of nothing now you can do to add to my comfort except to change your seat."

His face had reached such a climax of redness that it was one Glare. Mephistopheles always affects red. He Got him Behind me, and left me at peace with myself and all the world.

XXXIV.

SOMETIMES when I look back over the manuscript leaves of this book I am tempted to destroy it. Why? Why, because it would cut me to the heart if any reader should so misconstrue the spirit of this unpretentious volume as to believe that I had therein set myself up—or set any of the sitters at our Table or the Table itself up—as model characters. There is not a home in the land where happiness may not come and live as it lives in our home, if the occupants of that home will invite it, woo it, as we have done. There are homes far richer; whose attractions to the æsthetic sense are much more powerful than ours; where glorious picture galleries delight the eye of their owners; where superb statuary stirs their pulses to admiration of its grace; where leafy parks call them to poetic strolling; where blooming flowers of tropic climes flame their gorgeous hues and shame even that *chef d'œuvre* of your celebrated painter for which a fortune has just been paid. Our home would joy to have these things; but not having them, it *can* have that which these alone will fail to bring—and so can yours, reader, though your home be poorer still than ours.

If I have spoken lovingly of our dear ones—of our Rebecca, our Algie, our beloved W.—it is not because they have no faults to the eye which chooses to see faults, I suppose; but the eye of love does not so choose, and should not. Rebecca I maintain is one of the dearest women ever sent on earth to bless all those with whom she comes in contact; yet, I grieve to say, Rebecca is frequently reminded by a pain there, that she has a back. This you know is far from being the ideal woman we fain would have; and Rebecca says the next time she comes into the world she'll take my advice and go romp in the woods and jump off the barn and drive her father's cow home (the things W. did, she says), so that she'll be good and strong. Our Algie is the noble little fellow I have tried to picture him; a muscular, symmetrical juvenile gladiator, who is as strong as a young lion, and as gentle as a lamb. Affectionate, incapable of falsehood, hating what is wicked, adoring what is right, truly imbued with a beautiful religious spirit, he at the same time freely acknowledges that fun "suits him," and is so far removed from the wonderful young prig who is a model of all the virtues, social, religious, and scholastic, that it frequently has to be urged upon his attention that his heels, seen from an upper window as he throws somersaults over the area railings, are not pleasing to the eye of taste; and that in preparing his linen for the wash the introduction of two l's in the word "collars" would elucidate his meaning to the laundress. And our W.—what of him? No, no—not a word—not a breath, dear friends—*he* is faultless!

The true and only miscreant is I. I have already alluded to the Vesuvian character of my temper. Sarah Hoggins episodes enrage *me*, while all the rest of our folks are as smooth and unruffled as a placid stream. I am trying to improve myself in this regard. I am learning brave lessons from the beautiful equable characters of the noble people, for placing me among whom, God has my nightly thanks. Luther was a man of violent temper, but he curbed it. Temper is hideous in a woman. Every day I make these mistakes and I repent them in sackcloth and ashes. And I improve. Trifles have no longer the power to chafe me, as once they had; but never, I think, shall I succeed in vanquishing that hot rage which seizes me when weak and wicked men and women struggle to pollute the name of blessed Love, and kill the gentle household gods, which poor humanity so ill can spare.

Then do I thank God I have a voice which thousands upon thousands of people hear, every year. Then do I rejoice that, woman as I am, I load no Quaker-gun when I put pen to paper.

Sometimes those who love me remonstrate with me for spending my strength in fighting windmills. Is this Freelove monster but a windmill? Am I fighting nothing? Pray God it may be so. If it be, then many people of sound judgment are mistaken.

Our usually cool Rebecca is greatly agitated by it. "Are not girls frivolous enough, irresponsible, unthinking enough now? Shall they be urged to more weakness—more wickedness? Hitherto they have been pure at least—if no more."

Even sage W. shakes his head. "Bad teachings for the warm blood of our Algie—at this moment when he is about to enter manhood with all its temptations."

And just as we are talking, Algie runs in, screaming with laughter, and holding a copy of an illustrated paper in his hand.

"What's the matter, Algie?"

"Why look here," he says, "here's a picture of that nasty old Mrs. Freelove, and the artist has printed under it—

"'GET THEE BEHIND ME (MRS.) SATAN!'"

THE END.

www.ingramcontent.com/pod-product-compliance
Lightning Source LLC
LaVergne TN
LVHW010212110826
845151LV00004B/1068

9781425527952